The Deeper Journey
Companion Workbook

Ten Foundations for the
Sure-Footed Christian

DON VALLEY

The Deeper Journey Companion Workbook: Ten Foundations for the Sure-Footed Christian

Contents

Introduction

REPETITION AIDS LEARNING

I don't know who is responsible for that remark, but it is true. Also, I learned a long time ago about the value of physically doing something to secure the mental exercise while you are learning. This took on such practices as writing down an answer, or speaking it out loud. Also searching other sources besides what you have in hand serves to secure knowledge and understanding so it is not quickly forgotten. The intention for this workbook is to help you put into practical life the truths you so badly need to understand and live by. It will become an abbreviated reference for you to have when a question comes to your mind and you want the answer quickly and without having to search through a large book.

The Deeper Journey was conceived as a source a person could pick up and manage the understanding all by himself. This workbook is the companion to allow you to do the same. However, in a group gathering – a class at church, or a small group in the home – with a leader, your grasp of the materials will be deeper. You will sense greater confidence.

The church will find it to be a valuable tool in leading and training the new convert from the point of decision into a foundational understanding of the Christian faith. It is a great way to get the business of discipleship set in place for each person.

The book allows the subject matter to be conveniently arranged into the weekly class set-up, for the typical church calendar yearly schedule such as a Sunday school class or small group topic. It is suitable for both youth and adult groups.

Whether you are working through this resource independently or in a group setting, I pray the guidance of the Holy Spirit throughout as He brings you to understanding and to committing to live for Jesus Christ in every arena of life.

I bless you in the name of the Father, the Son, and the Holy Spirit

1st Foundation – Salvation: Your Eternal Destiny

My New Way of Life

I must be prepared in order to _____ myself from pressures and confusion that would take me

_____ and overwhelm me, leading me away from the new life I am to live.

Who Am I Now?

So you can get your "new you" engrained in your "new spirit" and secure your foundation, declare the following out loud at least once each day for a minimum of thirty days. Do it boldly and with confidence. Remember, you are doing warfare against satan and his army.

Declaration:

"I am a new creation in Jesus Christ. I am a re-born "babe" in Christ. I am a person of the Spirit, not a person of my old worldly nature any more. I still have a soul: my mind, will, and emotions. I respond with my spirit by the Spirit of God and to the Spirit of God. I now live and move and have my being according to the indwelling Spirit of God, and my very nature comes in line with the purposes and plans God has for me. Now I am equipped to live victoriously in the super-natural kingdom of God and enjoy my new home and territory in my Father's Kingdom here on earth.

What Am I Facing?

I am in a _____ against _____. He is the enemy of my _____

which Jesus has just _____. However, I can rest assured that I have _____

to fear. I am in the army that has just _____the _____. My Commander

in Chief is always with me to _____ and _____ when I ask. He loves me just as He

loves _____ _____. He will protect, preserve, and _____ me as I

grow and _____ into the person He has _____ me to be.

    A. I affirm, my decision is _____ in the Word of God! I understand satan will try to

make me _____ it was just an emotional _____not worthy of keeping.

    B. The new life I have chosen is not only worth living for, but also _____ for.

    C. There is no chance of _____ _____.

Now I Am a Believer

> ➢ *"For God so loved the world that He gave His only begotten Son, that whoever believes in Him should not perish but have eternal life." John 3:16* NKJ

When you see the "Arrow Point" symbol, this is a verse for you to commit to memory. John 3:16 is the first one for you to know and get deep down inside your spirit. These verses specified for you to memorize in this workbook – and many more in the full book – are necessary to give you unbreakable foundation in your Christian walk. Jesus spoke in one of His parables about the foolish man who builds his house on the sand. When the waves and winds came, it was destroyed. Then He refers to the wise man who built his house on solid rock. It withstood the ravages of the storms and was not weakened.

The same life principle applies here as you establish your sure foundation, getting key scriptures etched in your heart. At the times when you are challenged and would be tempted to doubt, there they are for you to use against the oppressor. Make a vow right now by saying:

"I will be diligent in committing to memory the scriptures I need for my foundation in Christ"

Let Me Help You

Perhaps you have never done scripture memorization before. Of course, you know that "repetition aids learning". It is actually quite easy when you go at it one at a time. First of all, here is one way: On small cards (such as 3x5") you can easily keep with you, write the reference on one side and the wording on the opposite side.

As you think of it throughout the day, read and say the scripture and the reference. Then as a few days have gone by, look at the words and speak the reference before you check it. Then, do the opposite: look at the reference and speak the verse. The idea here is to keep both the verse and the Bible reference identified together. As you add verses, keep making progress in the same way.

You will soon find the earlier ones just part of your regular thinking, immediately on your tongue. Also, to keep from having a bunch of cards shuffling around, it is good to punch a hole in the corner and put them on a snap ring, thereby you can arbitrarily flip through them from any point at any time. Maybe put a paper clip on the most recent so you are quick to find that one and then move on from there.

Salvation: It is a Gift from God

Salvation provides me with the gift of _____ _____.

The Greek word "sodzo" is translated as "salvation" which also incorporates _____,

_____, _____, and _____.

Jesus provided by His gift to me all the provisions I would need. It is not only the assurance of living through

eternity with Him, but all the _____ of life I am continuing here on earth. He did not send a

_____ for each thing we need. He gave total provision through His _____

_____ on the cross.

Key Truths Substantiating Your Salvation.

Truth: The name of _____ is the _____ name for salvation.

> ➢ **"Nor is there salvation in any other, for there is no other name under heaven given among men by which we must be saved." Acts 4:12**

There is no _____. It is absolute. Other opinions are part of satan's _____ tactics to keep me from choosing salvation. I recognize satan's aggression against me because he has lost me to God's kingdom. I am honored to know I have great _____ in God's kingdom and am moving into that. Philosophies and systems of religion not based on the Word of God – the Bible – will attempt to convince me of other ways to become a child of God. The Word of God given in the "Christian Bible" is the _____ Word of complete truth. I choose to _____ this truth, _____it, and convince myself of it, getting it _____ in my heart.

BELIEVE-RECEIVE: These are the requirements to be _____. Did you receive Jesus as your Savior? If you did, then YOU ARE A CHRISTIAN – a _____ of God.

> *"But as many as received Him, to them He gave the right to become children of God, to those who believe in His name."* John 1:12

> *"Believe on the Lord Jesus Christ and you will be saved."* Acts 16:31

Salvation By the Blood of Jesus
Truth: The blood of Jesus is what was provided to wash away your sins.

> *"And according to the law almost all things are purified with blood, and without shedding of blood there is no remission"* Hebrews 9:22

When you came to Jesus and _____ of your sin, it was washed away by the_____ of His blood.

Jesus was chosen by God – His Father – as a sin sacrifice. No other _____ made can help in removing any sin. Many people feel, because of the wickedness of their past that they must do something like paying _____ to help remove the guilt and pay for the depth of it. Jesus, having died on the cross – shedding His blood on your behalf – nothing else can _____. When you asked for forgiveness, it was _____. This may be hard to believe, but God, according to His Word, cannot _____ my sin anymore!!! When He looks at me He sees me through the _____ of _____ - washed and made whole.

5

The Old Covenant: (The Old Testament)

From the beginning, God established the law that there always had to be a blood sacrifice for sin. So specified animal sacrifices were made on a regular basis for all manner of sins. These offerings were made for His chosen people, the Israelites, to have their sins forgiven and be restored to fellowship with the Heavenly Father. This is the way it was done before Christ became the final sacrifice for mankind, once and for all. Any other _____ or _____ is not of God! Jesus was the perfect, _____ sacrifice. It is only through His _____ and His _____ we can acquire salvation. I have memorized Acts 4:12; it is proof.

Prayer For Salvation - Essential Ingredients

The Sinner's Prayer:

Father, in Jesus' name I _____ to You now to receive Your salvation. I know I have not lived life by Your standards; I _____ I am a sinner. I _____ of my sinful life and desire to make You my Lord and my Savior. So, I ask You to come into my heart; wash me clean by Your blood shed for me on the cross. I _____ Your name, Jesus, is the only name whereby I can be born again. I _____ right now Your acceptance of me as a child of Yours. I am born again. I am a new creation in Christ Jesus. Amen.

You have just filled in the "key essential Ingredients" for being accurate in making your confession complete.

Bible Verification

COME: Mark 6:37 - CONFESS: 1 John 1:9 - REPENT: Acts 2:38 - BELIEVE: John 3:36 - RECEIVE: John 1: 12, 13

Be certain you have covered all the bases. It is never wrong to repeat this sinner's prayer with someone else and, at the same time, reaffirming for yourself everything in it.

Follow Up to Salvation: Be Baptized in Water

As an _____Christian, I am to follow up my salvation by being water baptized. Of the several baptisms spoken of in the Bible, this is the first to come after you are saved. It is good to do it soon.

The Word is very explicit about the urgency of being baptized in water. The first "baptism" is the baptism of

_____. Then following closely is your baptism in _____. It is a sign and a

_____ of my choice to live as a follower of Christ Jesus.

Read the supporting story of Jesus' baptism:

      Matthew 3:13-17. Also, read Luke 3:16, Matthew 28:19, and Mark 1:4,5

Have you been previously baptized – perhaps as an infant? It is alright to be baptized again now that you have

come into a full _____ of the purpose. It is good to put your sign up again, letting others

know you are _____ and _____ with Whose you are.

The manner of baptism is not the issue; it is the _____. Jesus was laid down in the water and raised

up again. The explanation for this is the example of your being _____ with Christ and

_____ to new life. We can never be on more solid ground scripturally than doing what

_____ did in the _____ in which it was done.

Be baptized every one of you. This is not a _____ in God's Word; it is a directive – a

_____. I will walk either in _____ or rebellion.

The Big Benefit: Eternal life in heaven

It is not the "Big Benefit Theory – it is the ultimate _____ truth. When I consider the

alternative – eternal life in _____ - I will be encouraged through life's problems in order to achieve

this _____.

SLAM-DUNK!!! Jesus is the _____ living savior. No other _____ can make the

claim that _____ _____ lives!

When Jesus did what he had told His disciples all along, they were _____. However, the truth

had been so deeply _____ in them that they preached the _____

_____ message all around the world.   Jesus' second coming will _____

all other previous spectacular displays of God's _____.

Now, read in your Bible what you are to understand about Eternal Life:

Hebrews 9:28, 1 Thessalonians 4:13 – 18, Revelation 3:11,   Revelation 22:12, 1 Thessalonians 4:15 – 5:14

As you read these, dwell on what is spoken. Ask the Holy Spirit to bring understanding. Ask Him to cause you to

be deeply convinced of each truth.

> # And this is just the tip of the
> # "Iceberg" of Salvation

Now, be a living commercial: Be a witness

As a new child of God, born again by the Blood of Christ, there is nothing in all the world greater to tell another

about.   It is called _____. It is called spreading the _____. It is called

sharing the _____ _____ of Jesus.

The easiest way and _____ productive way is to share my _____.

Doing It: A Brief Word Script for You

I've developed a convenient pocket sized guide with the word script for you to follow. This is a simple tool for you to actually read. Of course, it is better to have it memorized and then use it only to check yourself to see that no ingredients have been missed. There is no greater joy in your Christian life than to accomplish bringing another lost soul out of the kingdom of darkness into an eternal relationship with Jesus Christ.

Beware of the Danger

Never leave the new-born believer without some ongoing help to secure his growth. If nothing else, your church bulletin will suffice. You can acquire copies of the book of John to give as a starter. Inquire of others as to creative ways they have to provide helps for the new Christian.

SALVATION INGREDIENTS	PRAYER FOR SALVATION
COME: "…and the one who comes to Me I will by no means cast out." – Mark 6:37 CONFESS: "If we confess our sins, He is faithful and just to forgive us our sins and to cleanse us from all unrighteousness." 1 John 1:9 REPENT: "Repent and be baptized every one of you . . for the forgiveness of sins" Acts 2:38 BELIEVE: "Whoever believes in the Son has eternal life, but whoever rejects the Son will not see life." John 3:36. RECEIVE: "But as many as received Him, He gave the right to become the children of God. John 1:12	Father, in Jesus' name, I come to You now to receive Your salvation. I know I have not lived by Your standards; I CONFESS I am a sinner. I REPENT of my sinful life. Now I desire to make You my Lord and Savior. So I ask You to come into my heart; wash me clean by Your blood shed for me on the cross. I BELIEVE Your name, Jesus, is the only name whereby I can be born again. I RECEIVE right now Your acceptance of me as a child of Yours. I am born again. I am a new creation in Christ Jesus. AMEN

Fold Here

2nd Foundation – Christlikeness

NOW THAT I KNOW, WHAT CAN I DO SO I CAN BE?

Your character as a Christian is to reflect the image of your Savior, Jesus Christ. Some, if not many changes will need to take place, showing your chosen new life to be genuine. Your life is a _____ of who you are as a child of God.

Declaration:
"I choose to prepare myself to face these changes with grace and thanksgiving. I will not be offended or insulted and will choose to face my needs and my lack with the confidence that the changes will make me into the child of God I desire to be above all else."

My Launching Pad Experience

I have come through the lift-off of salvation. I have been catapulted into unfamiliar territory. Yet I still have the right to make choices to have a life of joy, _____, health, happiness, and _____. Or I can choose to still experience _____ by wandering and experiencing the products of _____ satan wants for me.

My Launch

- My _____ was created
- My blueprint was worked to _____
- Jesus was the _____ for my lift-off
- My mission is accomplished, but not _____. Now the _____.

My Course – My Plan

Even though I am in new territory, I have the secure knowledge I will always be able to stay on course.

> **"I will instruct you and teach you in the way you should go; I will guide you with my eye." Psalm 32:8**

I am now under the total _____ of my Father's watchful eye

My Life From Here On

Stop right now. Get quiet and ask the Holy Spirit to come and be with you. In the spaces provided after each area, write one or more ways you sense the Holy Spirit's prompting you to improve and become more Christ-like.

- Fellowship with God daily:_____

  _____

- Fellowship with other believers:_____

  _____

- Right standing with my family:_____

  _____

- Responsible and accountable:_____

  _____

- Diligence:_____

  _____

- Disciplined: _____

  _____

- Self-discipline:_____

  _____

Read the Bible and Pray Daily

Prayer is _____ with God – Jesus – Holy Spirit. It is two-way. It is for me to not do all the _____. I must wait and _____ for God to talk to me. I have to discipline myself to be patient and _____ so I can know the _____ is communicating with me. In order to "steer my ship" I need to understand I never get all the _____ from the beginning. So I must be diligent daily by reading my _____ and praying.

> "Your word have I hidden in my heart, that I might not sin against You." Psalm 119:11

Your Beginning Process
- New Testament – Book of John – Read one chapter each day
- Old Testament – Book of Psalms – Read a chapter each day
- Your prayer time: Just talk to God – give Him praise and thanks – ask Him for His blessing – ask Him to meet needs you have – pray for His blessing on others – simply, listen to the things brought to your mind and then pray for them.
- Get quiet and listen – hear what God has to say to you. You may want to write it down.

After you have become seasoned and your private time in prayer is established, go ahead and set up your strategy according to your interests. I recommend reading the New Testament through and then going to the Old Testament and reading that through. Also, a daily devotional book in addition to your Bible time is a source of encouragement for each day. There are many. Go to your Christian book store and browse, asking Holy Spirit to point one out to you. Choose that one you keep being drawn to. (See Appendix D: Recommended Resources in the back of your *The Deeper Journey* book.)

Fellowship with Other Believers

"Let us not give up meeting together, as some are in the habit of doing, but let us encourage one another"
Hebrews 10:25

What You Surround Yourself With is What You Become

Having relationships with others of like faith is _____ to my keeping myself on target. If this were not necessary, God would not have placed my _____ for relationships in His Word. Realize, there is always the head of the _____ and the _____. Learn to be a _____ and to graciously be to _____ in the same way you need them to be there for you. Be _____. Be committed. Be yourself. Always go to church with the attitude, "I just came to _____ the Lord."

Take Your Part In Your Church Family

When you belong to a family, you have _____ by default. All members need to step up and be committed to _____. Church is a place where you _____ _____ and do your part.

Faithfulness in Attendance

It represents your _____ devotion to God. It is a great example to your _____ and others who are _____ at your life.

Faithfulness in Serving

There is no position more _____ than another. Find a place to serve and do it with _____. Jesus taught that the _____ in the kingdom is the one who _____.

Faithfulness in Giving

The greatest example of giving was God's gift of His _____, Jesus Christ – His _____. We worship God in the giving of our _____ and _____. The giving principle was established way back in the Old Testament when Abraham paid his first fruits – the _____ - to Melchizedek, the high priest. God trained the Israelites through the ages to bring their _____ _____ to the _____ for sacrifice and for supplying the _____ of those who _____.

Read Malachi 3:8-12. Focus on verse 10. Realize what the benefits are of being faithful in the tithe.

Look at it this way: God puts one hundred percent in your hand and blesses you with the over-abundant amount of _____ percent. God, in His mathematical creativity always makes _____ provision for you with the _____percent than if you keep the total amount. We love to receive the blessings promised through our father, Abraham. But wasn't that an Old Testament blessing? We can't pick and choose our areas of _____ and live in complete _____ and commitment as a child of God. The principle of giving is where your _____ is and is one of the highest forms of _____. Tithing and offerings must be an integral part of you in order for you to live in the fullest _____ of God's _____.

Be Careful of the Temptation to Go it By Yourself

You need guidance and protection at this particular time of vulnerability. You need good leadership and others around you who you can _____ and whose _____ you can emulate. Since no church is perfect, keep your eyes on God and the _____ principles of His Word. Never gauge your _____ by what you see in those who are not living by the _____ of truth and love. Love your church home and be a _____faithful part of it.

Be In Right Standing with Your Family

It is time to make those changes away from what you don't like about _____ and _____ you have been.

> ➤ *"Therefore, if anyone is in Christ, he is a new creation; old things have passed away; behold, all things have become new."* **2 Corinthians 5:17 NKJ**

You are a new _____ now. Walking in the "new you" must be your passion. Remember, your home is your launching pad; it is your _____ ground.

Helps for Living Out Your Change

In this listing of character natures, circle those positive ones. Underline those you are prompted to work on:

- ✓ Open and transparent   or   Private and closed
- ✓ Intolerant and judgmental   or   Work through difficulty
- ✓ Short-tempered, ill-mannered   or   Patient and loving
- ✓ Withhold love and affirmation   or   Express my feelings
- ✓ Grumpy and irritable   or   Joyful and cheerful
- ✓ Worried and restless   or   Trusting and peaceful
- ✓ Involved in wrongdoing   or   Enjoy doing right and good
- ✓ Hard and intolerant   or   Gentle and kind
- ✓ Easily angered   or   Well controlled
- ✓ Rebellious, belligerent   or   Honoring and peaceful

These characteristics are a good barometer to gauge your "old nature" and help you develop your "new nature" in the closeness of your home around those who know you best. You no longer go by the norms and pressures of the _____. To give you the picture of the new nature, read Galatians 5:22,23: *"But the Holy Spirit produces this kind of love in our lives:* **love, joy, patience, kindness, goodness, faithfulness, gentleness, and self-control."* Dwell on these characteristics and see yourself as this person in all its completeness. You can do it!!!

Be Responsible and Accountable

Your personality and _____ reflect the "real you". The extent of my ability to love others is indexed to my capacity to love _____.

Responsibility is a product of _____. Integrity is broken when some area is fractured or incomplete. Determine to make the needed changes. Living as a responsible believer positions me to be _____ for things whenever a _____ or _____ comes up.

- • **Truth and honesty:** Truth is the nature of Jesus Christ. Make this commitment: "I determine to be a person of my word. I will establish a reputation of _____ and trustworthiness. Others will know me as a person of great _____."

- **Accountability:** I will represent my choices without _____. I will be responsible to be accountable in every area and position I am responsible for. To be accountable is to be _____ in everything. I choose to be accountable and take complete _____.

- **Stewardship:** I choose to exercise good stewardship in all areas of my life: my household, my _____ life, my possessions, my _____, my body, my health, and so on. I will keep "careful care" of everything I have been given.

- **Honor:** I choose to respect and honor those in _____, knowing the same will be given back to me.

- **Attitude:** A positive attitude will always bring _____. Negativity breeds discontent and _____. In fulfilling my responsibility and staying _____ being _____ and _____, I will be in the right attitude and position in my Christian walk.

Declaration:

"Without leadership integrity, I cannot complete my mission. So, as to not deter my progress, I choose to be who I really am in Christ. I determine to walk this new walk with all I have in me. Now I am in the position where Holy Spirit can work in and through me greater understanding, confidence, and freedom."

Authority: Understanding It

Authority is the power behind the responsibility designated to you. Authority is a cascading structure: God – delegates authority to _____. Man then delegates _____ to others. Others delegate _____ to even others, and so on. The secure element in all this for you is knowing the authority you are under. With authority always comes _____. Therefore, I choose to uphold and _____ those in authority even when I would rather they do things differently than my _____ and _____. I choose to trust God to bring me to realize where I could be _____. I give the Holy Spirit _____.

God is my ultimate authority. I choose to stand strong in my places of authority, as well.

Diligence

Being diligent will bring me feelings of satisfaction and self-reward. I determine for diligence to be rooted as a character quality in my personality. It will keep me from procrastinating. It will cause me to be excellent in all things, not doing just enough to get by.

- DILIGENCE IN RESPONSIBILITIES: Ask yourself some questions here
  - Am I always on time?
  - Do I get to church a little early?
  - Do I plan ahead and give extra time for unforeseen happenings?
  - Am I typically late by waiting too long to get started?
- TIME USAGE
  - Do I get onto the task promptly?
  - Am I concentrating on what I am to do?
  - Am I dreaming about other things, such as quitting time?
  - Am I being diligent and responsible on this assignment?
  - Am I giving my best?
- CHORES AT HOME
  - Do I have to be reminded?
  - Do I keep good care of my home?
  - Does my car's appearance represent my Christian life?
  - Am I a good reflection of Jesus to others who see me and my surroundings?
- BALANCE – GIVE AND TAKE
  - Do I always want it my way?
  - Is what I want worth waiting for?
  - Do I put rewards before work?
  - Can I give in to others who need me?
  - Can I accept a gift as a blessing from God?

I am sure some of these questions caused an uncomfortable feeling to rise up. I challenge you to place a check mark in front of those you need to think through. Be honest with yourself. Knowing you are a work in progress, make strides to overcome the weaknesses you see. Then experience the freedom of diligence and its rewards.

Be Disciplined

Discipline is the reason you are working through the book and the workbook. You have chosen your desire for discipleship. Discipleship is the process of being _____, _____, instructed, and _____ in your choice of this "new-life-process". The discipleship process is for the purpose of establishing growth and maturity on a solid _____ that is unshakeable and _____. Like any structure, many different experts are necessary to provide excellence in _____ and _____ in order to build it so it will stand with absolute _____. Your new life as a child of God _____ the same attention.

- **First Discipline:** The Word of God. It is the _____ from which my discipline is to be developed

- **Second Discipline:** Others to disciple you. You need established Christians who are _____ in the local body of Christ.

- **Third Discipline:** Listen to teaching CD's and DVD's. There are areas of knowledge, interest and fulfillment needed in your understanding. They are specialized subjects out there to help _____ strengthen you. Unless you are taking charge and disciplining yourself to listen to and watch only what is _____ and _____, you are allowing the enemy to access your _____ through the world standards, and that is _____. The discipline here comes under the umbrella of _____ the mind. God never requires anything of you without it being for your ultimate _____.

Be Self-Disciplined: Manage your Character

In this personal area of living, the enemy would love to make you think these things do not have a scriptural specific to them, therefore this is deviation from the truth of the Word. That is why you must know there is no difference between something specifically addressed in the Bible and the character and nature of God's truths. The Bible tells us to be examples of Christ. So whatever you do and however you do it is an example of the Christian life. So, let's do a personal check to see how you stack up.

"How am I doing" is the question to keep in mind as you read and think through the following points.

- Prompt and timely
- Rules: resistant or compliant
- Anger: controlled, un-controlled
- Attitude: critical and negative or positive and encouraging
- Personal presentation: careless or careful
- Cleanliness: hygiene
- Personal interests: out of balance?
- Others: care for or unconcerned?

Promptness

Being on time is a _____ that says, "I can _____ on this person. He is _____ late and never gives _____." Not being on time is _____ to others. Maintaining _____ here is Christ like.

Promises

When you give your word, make sure you _____ it. Purposing to change and then walking in that purpose is _____ to your spirit. This is not legalistic, it is strengthening to your

_____.

16

Rebel Against Rules

Rules are for your protection and guidance. Your manner here is to _____, and better still – to

_____. Rebelling against a rule is saying, "I don't want to be told what to do." As a Christian, your

attitude must change to say, "I will _____ and _____ abide by the guidelines."

Do You Get Angry Quickly?

Anger jumps up because of something you _____. Anger comes from _____. Anger

is an _____ that must be brought under _____. Ask the Holy Spirit to help you.

Are You Critical of Others?

Being critical is in the same boat with _____. Read Matthew 7:1,2. This puts it into perspective so

you can choose to change a critical spirit. Speak gentle clear words of life and not _____ remarks.

Remember, there are _____.

Careless About Personal Appearance?

Appearance is the first _____ whereby a person will size you up. Our appearance says a

bunch about how much we _____. Your appearance is a barometer of _____ to

others. As a child of God, you _____ Him in how you keep yourself and keep what you have.

Determine to present yourself _____ with your clothing _____ and

_____.

Personal Hygiene

This area is _____ to be taken for granted. Poor hygiene is the area where you will experience

_____ more quickly than any other. We are talking about personal cleanliness. It may take

getting up several minutes earlier, but the _____ are worth more than the _____.

Time Management

This is about balancing your time between _____ and personal _____. It is about

priorities and putting first things first.

List items you can think of as basic priorities:_____

_____

_____

These are firsts for you to attend to. Now, what are some pleasures you enjoy that need to be managed in

addition to the basic priorities? _____

_____

_____

Outline and, then later, refine your plan for bringing balance so as not to "major on the minors".

Attention to Others

We reflect the character of Jesus as we _____ _____ to others. You need recognition, love, and acceptance. What does that say about others?   Choose to be more _____ to those around you. You are to be there for _____. Your _____ needs to know you are there for them.

Choose to Read Psalm 101 Aloud at the Beginning of Each Day

It will help you as you take charge in setting boundaries. It is a great covering for you as you bring your _____ in line with God's Word.

3rd Foundation – Prayer Life

MY DAILY TIME WITH THE FATHER

A Lifestyle Without Prayer is the Road to Certain Defeat!

Prayer is _____ with the Heavenly Father. It is the breath of your Christian walk. It is critical to your being able to living an _____ and _____ life.

Communication is a Two Way Street – You Talk, You Listen

This Is How

A. **First**

Get yourself a Bible you can easily understand. See the recommendation in Appendix D of your book. For you as a new Christian, I recommend one of the more contemporary translations such as the New International Version (NIV), New Living Translation (NLT), or the New American Standard (NAS). The authorized King James Bible is one to have in your collection, but is difficult for novices to understand and relate to because of the old language patterns.

B. **Next**

Choose an area of your Bible to settle into for the time. Avoid falling into the pattern of just arbitrarily flipping the book open and settling on whatever is there for your daily Bible time. This kind of approach produces an _____, easily discouraged and _____ believer with sketchy _____. Giving up is easy as a result. Have a plan that will keep your understanding in a growing pattern.   It is important for you, early on, to get comfortable with the _____ areas of God's Word. A good start is to begin with one chapter each day.

- First, start with the book of John
- Get a daily devotional book: See Appendix D in your book
- As soon as possible: Add into your day CD's with teachings on specialized topics to help you grow in the depth of your knowledge and understanding. These are like the fat around the muscle and bones of the structure.

Warning:

Over-enthusiasm can cause you to want to do it all in too short a time. Under the pressure of what you have put on yourself, defeat and discouragement can set in. Be _____ in your excitement. Do what you can _____ do. Pace yourself.

C. **Include Old Testament Reading**

Since the Old Testament is preparation for the Messiah – Jesus Christ, it is good to begin to have some understanding there, as well. The book of Proverbs or the book of Psalms are good starters. Psalms is a book of _____ experiences, full of _____ and comfort. If you are a person of historical interest, the books of Genesis and Exodus record God's nature and His _____ pursuit to have His children become _____ and _____ as a pure line in _____ His Son, Jesus, for us.

Protect Your Self

Protect Your Ear Gate: Music

It will, no doubt, be necessary to _____ your music choices. How does this relate to the area of prayer, you might ask. Well, by being in a constant attitude of prayer – communicating with God – at all times what you listen to throughout the day comes in through the ear and goes straight to your spirit. Changing your focus from the lyrics of the _____ stuff and _____ your spirit man with that which is godly and _____ is very important. It is time to put aside the interests of the _____ life and digest what is _____ and _____ for the spirit to grow on. Surround yourself with your faith _____ and become part of that community in all _____. Lean on those who are staid and mature Christians for your support, guidance and example.

Protect Your Eye Gate: Movies and Television

The Bible says: *"I will set no wicked thing before my eyes."* Ps. 101:3

You are not expected to watch nothing but Christian television channels and only Bible-centered movies. There is much available that is good clean entertainment that is enriching to your whole person. The challenge here is to establish boundaries within which you – as a growing child of God – choose to live.

If you are aware and awake today, you realize there is no secret about the intents of what the Hollywood thrust is against the _____ _____ of the United States with its motto – IN GOD WE TRUST. A constant diet of this type of movie with its violence, _____, foul language, and _____ exploitation will keep your mind occupied on that _____ of life, keeping you away from growing in _____ and _____. It takes no effort to turn on the TV and just watch whatever appears. It takes thought and effort to choose and stand by your choices – for you as well as those you are responsible for. Satan is very cunning. He wants you to _____ _____ the worldly areas of your _____ so you do not move into _____ in your Christian walk.

Take charge now and become all you can be as you build your godly character.

Have Your Intimate Prayer Time with the Father Each Day

This is a habit your entire being will soon come into complete agreement with. It must be firmly planted by unwavering diligence and become a _____ in your _____ _____.

The first several times, you may struggle with taking the time with Him whom you cannot see. As you get started in this new pattern of life, begin with ten or fifteen minutes and then let it grow from there.

- ✓ Establish your _____ to have your prayer time – some call it "quiet time".

   Make it _____ and uninterrupted. Prayer, in its simplest form is _____

   to God. Conversation is necessary in friendship, so learn to be _____ and hear His voice

   _____ to you. This is often the _____ part because we are uncomfortable

   with silence. As you focus on listening, you will begin to hear His still small _____ talking to

   you and telling you things He wants you to _____. Right here is a good plan to have

   _____ and _____ so you can jot down what He says to you. Remember, the

   stubbiest of _____ is better than the _____ of brains.

- ✓ Timing for prayer is important. Early morning is preferred. It can be a precious time of

   _____ with your Heavenly _____. There must be some private time in

   your day for your personal time with God. Choose whatever is best for you and _____ it

   into your schedule providing for no interruptions. Make it work. It will be the _____

   important _____ each day.

Prayer Pattern

Read Psalm 100:4. This is always a good pattern to follow giving you confidence you are in good standing. Your prayer can be silent. God, being all-knowing, reads your thoughts.

Write a list in each of the following to have as a good reminder:

- ✓ Thanksgiving and Praise:

   _____   _____   _____

   _____   _____   _____

- ✓ Pray for Others:

   _____   _____   _____

   _____   _____   _____

   _____   _____   _____

- ✓ Your Country:

   _____   _____   _____

   _____   _____   _____

Memorize Psalm 51:10-12. This is a fantastic way to bring cleansing to your soul and spirit right at the start of each day.

Be Still and Listen

This part of prayer time seems the most difficult to get into. It is called _____ prayer. On the advanced – longer time frame – it is called _____ prayer.

At this point you become silent and listen with your _____ to hear that quiet voice speaking to you. You must take charge of wandering in your thoughts and command them to be still. You will find His voice to be loving, _____, helpful, bringing fulfillment into what is _____ for you today.

Start with just _____ minutes. Hold on; you are in _____. New habits are always difficult to get seated. _____comes into play here. After several days, go to _____ minutes; this takes you deeper. From there your desire for that quiet time hearing the Father's voice will grow in _____ and _____. Your appetite for it will increase.

Pray Without Ceasing

This means to be in a prayerful attitude throughout the day.

Positions and Conditions

Kneeling is Not Necessary for Prayer

Kneeling is a posture of _____ and respect and is good. When you go to your "prayer closet" – your place of private prayer – you may want to kneel, you may wish to sit in a specially comfortable chair. It makes no difference. That place and posture providing the environment for intimate relationship with the Father is the right choice for you.

Closing Your Eyes is Not Necessary

God saying we should pray without ceasing in no way indicates we should _____ or close our eyes. The actual intent of this is to be in a _____ _____ of prayer. This is the best way to keep your mind from wandering into the _____ thought life satan would use to _____ you. God has given you this marvelous tool for your protection.

You Don't Have To Move Your Lips

God, and only God, is omniscient (all-knowing) and is able to read the _____ and intents of your

_____. So, you do not have to speak out loud when you pray.

The enemy hears only what is spoken out loud – he is not omniscient. The air is his _____. When

you speak you _____ the molecules and disturb those _____

_____ - the atmosphere. It gets his _____ and the power of your words

takes _____ over him.

In a group environment, praying aloud at times will be needed so others can come into agreement with what you

are praying. Prayer is "simply" talking to God. Your Heavenly Father hears you pray just as you _____

to anyone else around you. Special kinds and types of _____ are completely unnecessary. Just speak

to God as you would to _____ else in the group. You don't have to _____ your prayers

to be perfect; just be comfortable with _____ to God no matter when and where it is.

Prayer Types

Thanksgiving – Praise – Petition – Intercession – Supplication – Listening – Faith – Consecration – Agreement

Be at ease. You are not expected to cover all these areas of prayer every time you have your daily private time

with your Heavenly Father. Now, isn't that a relief?! You are just to be sensitive to the _____

voice of the Holy Spirit. During your day, you may sense the need to intercede for someone He brings to mind. Or

you may feel impressed to _____ a part of your life to your Lord right as a certain time.

As you go through your day, remember that casual _____ is being disobedient or

disrespectful to God. It speaks of a very personal and _____ relationship with the Father.

✓ **Thanksgiving and Praise**

List some things to offer to the Father here:_____

_____

_____

✓ **Petition Prayer**

This is the asking part. This is where most people _____ and end.

The Father loves to have you make your _____ so He can respond back to you. That is how He

shows His personal _____ for you.

Read III John: 2 and dwell on it. Read Philippians 4:19 and dwell on it. Read 1 John 5:14, 15 and dwell on it.

In all these verses you can see how your Heavenly Father desires your best while at the same time requiring you to believe and exercise your faith.

Also, your Heavenly Father loves you too much to give you what you want when He knows you cannot _____ it yet. He loves to see His children _____. So don't be shy about _____. However, be careful to not make asking for _____ the sole content of your _____ each time you come to your special prayer time. Prayer is a time of establishing your _____. Christian living is about _____. God is moved by your prayers. It is not a religion; religion is _____; it is _____. Relationship is encompassing and yet _____.

✓ **Intercession**

This means to pray for, in _____ of someone or some peoples or some _____. It is an intensive work in prayer as you _____ and prevail, beseech and cry out. Usually a person _____, after a time of intercession, a certain moment of _____ when the need to continue is over.

As you are prompted to pray for _____ who comes to mind, _____ allow yourself to disqualify God's voice. You can intercede silently wherever you are and whatever you are doing.

✓ **Supplications**

This is more of an attitude or manner of praying. An attitude of _____ and even quietly weeping in earnest speaks of this type of prayer. It is not _____ or anemic; it is quiet and _____ with great sincerity.

✓ **Listening**

It is termed "Soaking Prayer" by some, and that is a great description. It is going into a time of prayer without _____ anything!! Think about and then write what kind of posture you would place yourself in for this type of prayer. Remember to have a pen or pencil and a pad to write down what you hear God saying to you.

✓ **Faith – Agreement – Consecration**

Faith: Read Romans 4:7 KJV. This sums up the prayer of faith. In your prayer of faith, you come into

_____ with what you are trusting for and then you _____ God for what you have

prayed for. When you speak in prayer, you set in motion at that _____ God's power to

_____ and bring about the object of your prayer. Even though the answer may not be

_____ right away, the actuality of it is _____.

Agreement: This is when you _____ yourself and join in with the prayers of another person or

group. It is very powerful. Read Deut. 32:30. The enemy tries to make you think he is more

_____ than he really is. The power in you is far _____ than

_____ satan can try to scare you with. When you have overwhelming difficulty, have

_____ join you in the prayer of _____.

Consecration: With contrite heart and firm resolve, you stand firm in the dedication or _____

you have been brought to present before God.

Write down a few areas of consecration in your life to put before God for eternity.

_____

_____

_____

Prayer fuels your tank, providing _____, _____, and sustaining _____.

You really cannot live a consistent _____Christian life without _____ prayer. It

really isn't how much; it is the _____ of it.

Declaration

> "Father, I purpose to talk with You every day, not as a duty but as a desire. I choose to be diligent and
> enjoy the results of having my special time with You. I honor You in all areas of my life and determine
> to succeed in this very intimate area. Help me to know how to love You and to realize You are my
> personal Father, wanting those intimate times with me. I desire for You to increase my fellowship with
> You every day."

4th Foundation – Checkpoints

GUIDEPOSTS FOR LIVING LIFE

Everyone needs to have a gauge for life's practices. Standards and practices acceptable to those around us are important to our Christian way of living as we display the genuineness of Christ Jesus and how He lived and circulated right here "where the rubber meets the road".

Checkpoints are situations and circumstances you encounter where you need _____ and _____. Actually, this is the process of _____.

Understanding Sanctification

Sanctification is the process of growing in _____ and _____. Read Phil. 2:12. As you dwell on this scripture, you will probably determine you are a work still in progress. You still have much to bring under the _____ of Christ.

Jesus was sinless. However, we – having been born in sin – have a long line of _____ sin and _____ pressuring us. When you became a child of God, that was your new birth in the realm of the _____; your spirit was reborn. At that time your soul: your _____, _____, and _____ was not perfected.   There is still a lot of residue from the sinful _____ to be brought into _____ to the _____ of Jesus Christ. So this is what "working out your salvation" refers to, that is, sanctification. When Jesus said, "It is finished" on the cross, it did not mean there was no more work to be done. What was being said was that the plan and _____ God had prepared was not complete. Now, using the _____ the _____ could be read, understood, and used to bring about the actual _____ drawn up by the Master Planner.

Until a blueprint has the official stamp, signed and dated, it is not _____ as finished. The blueprint for man was _____ and _____by Jesus' death on the cross. Therefore, God's _____ for mankind is complete. Now you are to use the plan to become _____ in Him.

This is not about good works in order to gain salvation. Read Eph. 2:8-10. Your salvation is in place. It is about bringing all areas of your life into _____ _____ so you can live your life free and _____.

The Proper and the Good

How am I to represent Jesus Christ in everyday normal living?

- *Mingling with people*

  Write eight or more personality qualities in this area:

  _____

  _____

  _____

  _____

  _____

- *Manner of Dress*

  What is the dress code for the Christian?_____

  Name several acceptable dress mannerisms of worldly standards._____

  _____

  _____

  Remember, you can be very much in fashion and "cool" without _____ to the extremes of the

  world.

  For the lady: What is revealed before the _____ of a boy or man is perceived as being

  _____ and that _____ is to come.

  Remember, for both the man and the woman, tight clothing revealing every curve and tuck of the body is

  _____ and _____. You must make your choice to either live by the

  "bible of the _____" or by God's _____.

- *Relating to People*

  As a believer, you are not an _____ unto yourself. In your relationship with others you have

  _____. Each person you encounter deserves _____ and respect.

  You must see each person as having a soul just as _____ as yours.

  - **At Home:**

    I am to honor my_____

    _____

    Mannerisms for me to display at home:_____

    _____

    Improper characteristics I must check myself on:_____

    _____

    Simple recognition of a person says: "_____" I must

    develop this _____ in my home in order to be that way in all other places.

- **At Work or School:**

  God has _____ figures everywhere. The attitude of being resistant and

  disrespectful prevails presently throughout society – even in the _____. God's

  authority structure is for your _____.

  Write down the authority figures in the various areas of your life right now:_____

  _____

  _____

  _____

  Write down those people over whom you have authority:_____

  _____

  _____

  _____

  Each level of authority carries responsibility to a certain _____ and then comes under

  authority. To put your mind at ease, God is your _____ authority in every

  situation.   Those as your immediate oversite are in your life as _____ authority for you

  in that environment. You are to place yourself _____ their authority as unto

  _____.

  Now write down your response to the big question:_____

  _____

  _____

- **Responsibility:**

  You are to be responsible and care for whatever you are given in _____arenas of your

  _____.   Responsibility is yours to handle in all places and things where you have been

  given _____.

  With authority comes _____.

  You are held _____ for your responsibility.

  The four virtues I am to have as patterns as I walk in my given authority:

  1._____   2. _____

  3. _____   4._____

  Write down one or more areas of personal challenge as you read Eric's story: _____

  _____

  _____

  _____

o **Social Graces:**

These are pleasing and proper manners reflecting your _____ _____ as you inter-act with others. These must be learned and solidified in your _____ so you are not perceived as being _____. Genuineness and _____ are both read quickly. Personality mannerisms are not something to use to get an _____ with others. They are the same in the home with your _____ as well as all other circumstances. This whole area refers to developing _____ behavior and all times. The _____ you.

Here, I will start a sentence in each of the "bulleted" areas; you are to finish it out

- One little word is _____
- Acknowledge _____
- Respect_____
  Develop the _____
  When you don't know_____
- Keep _____
  Whenever you make a_____
  Bottom line: Do you want_____
  _____
  _____
- The first requirement: _____
  A "Thank You" note _____
  Birthday: A card _____
  It says to that _____
  _____
  Christmas: Gifts given do _____
  Excessive giving _____
  The pleasure of each moment_____

- o **Visits in homes: Special reminders**
  - First: _____
  - Dress _____
  - A gentleman _____
  - Use the front door:_____
  - Hostess gift:_____
  - Be on _____
  - Conversation: Make it _____
  - Children: Keep _____,
  - Cell phones. Turn them _____.
  - It is discourteous_____
  - Sometimes you are_____
  - Express _____

What does this all have to do with being a believer?

Remember, Jesus was the great example of a _____; when He was in a mix of people He was fully _____ and always _____ of those _____ Him.   You are to find where you can _____ and _____ the joy of being like Jesus in that personality trait.

Growing UP - Maturing

As you read through Brent's story, no doubt some promptings came to you. Write them here as reminders of commitments you choose to make.

_____

_____

_____

_____

Deception: believing that circumventing what is _____ will bring _____results than _____ what is right.

Brent had it backwards. His children are wanting to follow his example. When God does a work He

_____ brings greater _____ than we can think or imagine. Proof of all this takes

considerable time when life patterns and attitudes are so deeply rooted. Nevertheless, God is always

_____ to His Word.

Commit to Memory:

> ➤ *"Have I not commanded you? Be strong and courageous. Do not be afraid; do not be discouraged,*
>
> *for the LORD your God will be with you wherever you go. Be strong and of good courage, for the*
>
> *Lord, thy God, is with you."* Joshua 1:9

Life as a child of God is an _____ and a _____. The product of change for the

better brings a sense of _____ and value. Even though some things come more

_____ than others, the end result is _____ for your _____ and for your

pleasure – ultimately God's _____ for you. **JUST DO IT!**

5th Foundation – Solid Truth

ESSENTIAL ANCHORS FOR YOUR FAITH

Creeds and belief systems – oaths and vows. These are all part of securing your faith in a new direction a person takes when committing to another focus for his life.

As a Christian, you must determine to grasp and never let go of the truths established in and securing you in that life commitment. Otherwise, you will waiver and consider the _____ of other strains of belief. You must _____ to not _____ from the _____ you have chosen to live by. There must be no _____, additions, or _____. Solid faith brings unbroken life. It goes far beyond the choice to adopt a new _____ of

_____.

Your Cardinal Doctrines

The Apostle's Creed is our hard-core _____ _____ in a nutshell.

Recite this creed aloud daily until it gets rooted solidly into the fiber of your spiritual being. This is who you are as a person of the Spirit, not of the flesh. This creed is where you go when you want to know exactly the

_____ of what your faith-based belief system is. By making these declarations often, you serve to firm up your spiritual _____ just as a weight lifter does in the physical.

APOSTLES' CREED

To secure firmly your belief system from the very start, finish each of the twelve points of the following:

1. I believe in _____

   _____

2. And in _____

3. Who was _____

4. Suffered under _____

   _____

5. The third day _____

6. He ascended_____

   _____

7. From thence _____

8. I believe_____

9. I believe _____

10. The _____

11. The _____

12. And _____

The Bible is the Holy-Spirit _____ words of God through obedient _____ who

recorded it over a time span of many years. While many have tried to dispute the truth of the writings,

_____ has there been any _____ in this.

Right now choose to establish your commitment as a complete believer with this declaration:

> **"My faith is established in the Word of God lodged in my heart; I believe God's Word is the only source of truth, and nothing can cause me to waiver from that."**

A Bible Look at Each Point

Now, with your Bible, turn to the scriptures given and read through them

1. **I believe in God the Father almighty, maker of heaven and earth.**
    Genesis 1:1
2. **And in Jesus Christ, His only son, our Lord**
    1 John 4:9, 1 Cor. 8:6
3. **Who was conceived by the Holy Ghost, born of the virgin Mary**
    Mat. 1:18
4. **Suffered under Pontius Pilate; was crucified, dead and buried: He descended into hell**
    Mat. 27:28-30, Luke 23:46
5. **The third day He rose again from the dead**
    Luke 24: 5-8
6. **He ascended into heaven, and sits on the right hand of God the Father Almighty**
    Mark 16:19
7. **From thence He shall come to judge the quick and the dead**
    Acts 10:42
8. **I believe in the Holy Ghost**
    John 14:26
9. **I believe in the holy catholic* church; the communion of saints**
    Eph. 5:23, Hebrews 10:25
10. **The forgiveness of sins**
    Acts 10:43, I John 1:9
11. **The resurrection of the body**
    I Cor. 15:42, 44
12. **And life everlasting** John 6:47, John 3:16[1]

---

[1] * The word "catholic" can be confusing, but actually means "universal". It is not capitalized Catholic Church.

What's Right? – What's Wrong?

Let's Go For It!

- Right is _____ what lines up and is in keeping with _____.
- Wrong is anything out of line with God's _____, His character, His _____
- There are no gray areas – fence straddling - _____ with God
- To live in right relationship _____ guarantees _____
- To live aside from God's plans and purposes for you results in _____
- God's _____ does not permit _____ _____wrongful practices.

The earliest explanation of what was set before us as right and wrong were the ten _____.

God is, and always was, a _____ God who left no leeway for _____ on the

issues. The sooner you buy into that and place it into every _____ of your being, the greater the

_____ you will live in.

Jesus said He did not come to destroy the works of the law, but to fulfill them. Read Matthew 5:17. So the right

and wrong of the laws of the Old Testament are still yours to walk in today. They are for all peoples for all time.

The Ten Commandments proclaim a lifestyle _____ endorsed by God. They are the perfect

expression of _____ God is and how He wants _____ to live. Although a specific law may

not apply to us today, the timeless _____ or principle behind the law does. The principles and

natures of the Old Testament law still _____ through _____ and life in Him.

The story of the Ten Commandments and how they were given to Moses by God is exciting. Read through Exodus,

chapter 19 to see why they were necessary.

Take the attitude that the Ten Commandments are a set of simple requirements by your Heavenly Father that are

good and practical standards to live by. In the following, after each personalized commandment statement, speak

aloud the commitment you are establishing in that specific area.

Let's Personalize the Ten Commandments

1. I ACKNOWLEDGE YOU, GOD, AS MY LORD AND MY GOD WHO BROUGHT ME OUT OF MY TROUBLES

    - Realizing You, God, Saved me - - - -

2. I CHOOSE TO HAVE NO OTHER GODS BEFORE YOU, O GOD

    - I choose from this day - - - -

3. I SHALL NOT MAKE FOR MYSELF ANY IDOL - AN OBJECT – A PERSON. I WILL NOT BOW DOWN TO THEM

    - I will not allow - - - -

4. I WILL NOT MISUSE THE NAME OF THE LORD MY GOD BECAUSE YOU WILL HOLD ME GUILTY IF I DO

    - I will not use Your name - - - -

5. I WILL HONOR THE SABATH DAY AND KEEP IT HOLY AS A DAY OF REST AND NOT LABOR

    - I will set aside - - - -

6. I WILL HONOR MY FATHER AND MOTHER SO THAT I MAY ENJOY LONG LIFE ENJOYING THE REWARDS AND BENEFITS OF THINGS GOING WELL IN EVERY AREA OF MY LIFE

    - I will always honor - - - -

7. I WILL NOT KILL ANYONE

    - I will not kill - - - -

8. I WILL NOT STEAL FROM ANYONE – PERSON OR ORGANIZATION

    - What belongs to - - - -

9. I WILL NOT LIE AGAINST OTHERS – I WILL ALWAYS TELL THE TRUTH

    - Knowing the lie - - - -

10. I WILL NOT WANT WHAT OTHERS HAVE – POSSESSIONS, GIFTINGS, ANOINTINGS, ETC

    - I will not envy - - - -

These choices you make every day of your life are the power to _____ in your warfare against the enemy.

Declaration:

> **"Father, I choose as of this very moment to accept and live by the principles and truths in Your Word. I will gauge my living by Your solid guidelines for me and be confident that, through Jesus who lived by what You said, I can live a life pleasing to You. That is my desire."**

6TH FOUNDATION – FAMILY UNITY
FAMILY LIFE

The family unit is the most powerful force against the enemy because it is God's _____ in the _____ realm to pattern the _____ structure whereby He designed His plans for all creation.

The key scriptural principle for the family is God's established plan and order of authority. Write these for yourself as you choose to live with unbroken integrity in this principle:

_____   _____   _____   _____   _____

Always remember who is first, then next, then next, etc. Satan wants to invade this by bringing _____ and _____.

Once you are walking in right relationship between you and your Heavenly Father, you are in place to live in _____ with your family.

You: The Son – The Man – The Husband – The Father

You are always a _____. As you understand this, there are building blocks that create your wholeness as a son.

Obedience

Obedience is the nature of Jesus Christ. If you want to be like Jesus, you must be willing to be _____ to your parents, no matter what your _____ is. God placed you in just the _____ family. Only through His planning it _____ way and you walking in obedience – whether you like it or not – are you able to _____ His _____. God will bring His best to you as you _____ to His will. All of this disqualifies the "but I know best" attitude.

Attitude

A good attitude provides _____ and _____. A good attitude is a _____ you make, a commitment you choose for yourself. When you do not like what you are hearing, having a _____ attitude through the working-out _____ will cause you to gain good ground.

Respect

Respecting the other members of your family is a _____ _____quality. Respect is shown when you _____ speak about any member of your family in a derogatory manner. To tear another down with _____ is to bring yourself even _____ in the eyes of others.

Honor

Honoring your father and mother is _____ _____ for things to go well with you. It is to identify with their _____ as the parents God gave you. Whether or not you think they are honorable does not come into play here.   Remember, in some situations we honor out of _____, not out of _____.

Write several authority figures in your life right now:_____

_____.

Your check: If things are not going well for you, check your honoring attitude.

Honesty

To be accountable is to own up to anything you are _____ for. If you do not keep your room in order, for example, are you willing to be held accountable for it?   You will be required at home, and through life, to give an _____ for each area of responsibility. Your home is your training and proving ground.

Thankful

Be genuinely thankful for what you have, no matter what others _____ to have that may seem _____ or more _____.   IF YOU ARE NOT THANKFUL FOR WHAT YOU _____, YOU WILL NOT BE THANKFUL WHEN YOU _____ MORE. Thankfulness is a _____ and so is un-thankfulness. Your right to be thankful is not _____ by more or less. God wants your _____, too.

Choices

Accept the plan God is bringing you through and learn to _____ with it. All of the choices are churning around in that _____ at once. These are times to trust and choose to be _____ in what you know to be right and not trust in your _____ feelings.

Choose to be comfortable with _____ God has you to be _____.

The Right Choices Right Now

Make these your declarations:

I Choose to . . .

- ✓ Walk in_____
- ✓ Commit to _____
- ✓ Live_____
- ✓ Talk with_____
- ✓ Determine _____
- ✓ Keep a _____
- ✓ Spend some _____
- ✓ Keep the_____
- ✓ Be _____

As a son living according to these choices, you will be respected, honored, desired, and loved by your other family members as well as others wherever you are.

Girls and You

Every normal young man eventually gains a heartbeat that is attracted to girls. This is good and right. God _____ it to be that way. The right and wrong of it is _____ you deal with your attraction. The pressure to be accepted and "cool" can _____ you if you have not established _____ _____ to live righteously by God's standards.

Your safety factor is in making concerted decisions - _____ _____ to have in place before ever encountering an experience you don't know how to handle.

These are to _____ you from entertaining _____ that come up and _____ to them and then being sorry afterwards when it is _____ _____.

As a child of God, you have been given a spirit of _____. It is the knowledge of the difference between _____ and _____. You must be keen to the point that you realize the _____ you are _____ will over-ride that voice of discernment if you allow it to. This is the reason to make vows far in _____ of events and situations you may come to; you have the voice of the _____ _____ reminding you of your _____ - your choice. The strength to do what is right _____ up inside you and you walk away from _____ to something that could make a permanent _____ on your _____.

Concerted Decisions – Vows

Make them yours right now …

- ✓ Any girl I date _____
- ✓ I will not be _____
- ✓ I will never _____
- ✓ I will never submit_____
- ✓ I will never engage_____
- ✓ I will pursue _____

The Big Choice: Choosing Your Wife

Choosing your life partner is the second in importance to your choice to be a Christian. Your feelings of love and fascination are not _____ to make this decision. You must solidly depend on knowing God's _____ and your determination to _____ with Him in this.

Helps for Wisdom in Making Your Decision

Learn To Know Her Family

Write a list of characteristics to watch for in her relationship with her family. _____

_____

_____

Because she has had life modeled to her by her family, her family life is what she will _____ into the marriage as _____ and example.   The ploy of the enemy wants you to think that once you get married all the _____ will change and you will life in bliss.   Life mannerisms are very deeply _____ and will grow the same _____, no manner where it is planted. If you walk in the joy of the Lord yourself, you will have the _____ to do what is _____ in _____ circumstance and recognize God's _____ moving in your life.

Your Engagement – Not Too Extended

The engagement time is the arena for getting to really _____ know _____, _____ and friends of your fiancé. During this time, going for inner healing personal wholeness ministry will help you to keep from dragging unnecessary _____ into your married life. The early months and years of marriage are _____ enough in growing together through your new relationship without having to deal with issues of _____ _____ and _____ _____.

YOU – THE HUSBAND

The joy of experiencing the love you give to your wife and the pleasure of receiving from her is God's gift to you. This is right. This is good and desirable in the plan of God for you.

Now God steps in Here with Some Pointed Instructions

Read and digest Ephesians 5:23-33 – all eleven verses.   Then take a good hard look at what this means for you to live by.   Since you are a _____ being, what is practical is also under the _____ of your spirit man, because the way you relate to others _____ your relationship with _____. You have been _____ by God as the head of your family just as He is the head of the _____. The church is the _____ _____ _____ throughout the world. Write down how you perceive God:_____ Now you know what your place is as the _____. By you staying in right relationship before your Heavenly Father, the results will be as He has _____ for you.

The three specifics of commitment to your wife are:

1. Love your wife _____
2. Separate yourself_____
3. Leave bitterness_____

Your character qualities are no _____ within the boundaries of _____ than they are in the development of your own personal _____.

In those times when stress and misunderstanding set in, your understanding of being the "head" will be _____. Go to the end of the parallel chapter in your book and insist on going through the steps in CONFRONTATION WITHOUT AGGRAVATION. It is just as right for _____ as it is for her.

Critical Areas in Keeping Her Content

✓ _____

✓ _____

✓ _____

When you think about these three areas, you see the underlying _____ of the _____, _____, and the _____.

✓ The _____ is always speaking to you

✓ The _____ will never leave you or forsake you

✓ The _____ Through Him we are always sensing his touching and approval.

YOU AS FATHER

Fatherhood is not taught; it is _____. How you live before your children is how they will

_____.

God Disciplines

The way He does this is _____. He set up his benefits by agreement, giving two sides to a

situation. This is called _____. He will always keep His side; it is up to you to

_____ your side.

Love is Discipline and Discipline is Love

Out of guilt, we tend to be too _____ with our children's guidance, _____ the

freedom they have and the _____ we get them will _____ what they

_____ in their absence from you as their dad. Beloved, NOT SO! They must see your firmness in

a _____ and _____ way. Children see the lack of discipline as a lack of _____,

_____, and _____.

Discipline is not _____. Discipline is caring guidance with _____.

Read what God says in Proverbs 22:6 KJV. Children are molded into great citizens through this type of

_____ training. Meaningful time you spend with your children is mostly just you having them

_____ you. Just allowing them to be with you and making them feel like you _____ them

there is the most important. Children model what they _____. Living life is _____ not

_____. Your example speaks stronger than any _____ of _____.

Caught in a time crunch? You can't do everything you feel pressured to do. So what you need to do - in every

situation – is talk to the _____ _____ - to the Father – to _____.

The Holy Spirit is _____ there to help and comfort.

YOU: THE GIRL – THE DAUGHTER – THE WIFE – THE MOTHER

Much could be repeated because it applies to you. So, rather than be redundant, I ask you to turn back a few

pages and work through the BUILDING BLOCKS: Obedience – Attitude – Trust – Honor – Honesty – Thankfulness.

These life qualities are the same for you as for a boy. The uniqueness with which God made the girl is

_____ to Him, and you must _____ that special _____ God has

for you.

You as a Young Christian Lady

Now, you are experiencing physical changes and a new shape to your body. This unique person God is making you

to be must be someone you _____. Rather than yielding to the societal trends that idolize

_____ _____ portrayed by _____ models, choose to be pleased with

the _____ God has _____. If you look at _____ in reference

to others you admire, you will always be _____.

Never try to be like _____ else. It is impossible. It is futile. It is _____. Enjoy God's

beautiful _____ and make Him proud of how you _____ of His little girl.

Right Here - Right Now - The Right Choices Once Again

I Choose to . . .

- ✓ Walk in_____
- ✓ Commit to _____
- ✓ Live_____
- ✓ Talk with_____
- ✓ Determine _____
- ✓ Keep a _____
- ✓ Spend some _____
- ✓ Keep the_____
- ✓ Be _____

Boys and You

The girl – being a daughter – gets her idea of what a man is by the _____ of her dad. In a home without a dad, she will identify with some _____ _____ to live before her what a man is. Your attraction to boys will reflect that _____ you see in that father _____.

As you are pursued by boys, remember first and foremost who you are in _____. This will always guide you to be more keen in seeing _____ motives for a relationship. You must stand strong and understand that a young man's kindness and _____ can also be used in a _____ way. All desires for a relationship are not always_____. Trust the Holy Spirit to give you _____ and _____; then hold onto it.

By making concerted _____ months and years in advance of potential situations, you can _____ yourself from getting _____.

Concerted Decisions – Vows

Complete these vows as you prayerfully make these ahead of time
- ✓ Any boy I date _____
- ✓ I will not _____
- ✓ I will never _____
- ✓ I will never _____
- ✓ I will never engage_____
- ✓ I will pursue _____

Beauty – it is in How You Represent Yourself.

Your true beauty is in your _____ relationship with God. It is in your _____, not in your _____ choices. The more flesh a boy sees, the more he _____ to see and get _____ with.

So How Can I Be An Example of Genuine Beauty?

- **Be Modest**

   Modesty reflects your _____ and _____ about who you are and all that you really are.

   Never adapt to the standards of the world as your _____ and _____.

   Clothing styles for the ladies today promote _____.

Three questions bringing compromised choices:

- ✓ How far do I dare let my neckline _____?
- ✓ How _____ can I wear my skirt?
- ✓ How _____ tight can I stand to wear my clothes?

When you purchase your clothes with these questions in mind, you appear sadly _____, _____, and _____. Gaping necklines, short skirts, and tight-fitting revealing clothes are not _____.

A good guideline for modesty is:

- ✓ Hemline _____
- ✓ Neckline _____
- ✓ Clothing fit _____

God has given you those feminine _____ to _____ for the best He has for you – your future husband. You will not attract a _____ man by exposing what is to be _____ from the eyes of those around you. The real man loves that _____ quality in a woman and is attracted to your _____ beauty, not by over-exposed _____ fleshiness.

If you have to be like the crowd to be popular, you are associating with the _____ crowd. Your popularity is not determined by your appearance; it is determined who you truly are in your _____ and how you _____ to others because of your _____ with that. Most young people, if not all, are looking for exactly what you have. Soon, you will realize others will _____ you and begin to _____ you seeing something _____ in you they can identify with. Your popularity is far greater than the _____ popularity the _____ would entice you with.

- **Grace**

  Your mannerisms will show others whether or not you display _____ and _____. Grace comes from internal _____ and being certain of who you are and _____ you are. As you reflect the Jesus in you, you will not be _____, _____, _____ and intolerant. This does not mean you stand for abuse. The strongest statement is to _____ yourself and not

succumb to any kind of abuse. Grace never is identified in _____.

- **Charm**

  Charm is a strong element of _____ and is depicting of a true lady in

  _____. Your charm is not there for _____. Charm is

  displayed both in the _____ of your dress and the _____ of your

  countenance.

- **Personality**

  Do you desire to show _____ and be charming? Or do you want to be _____

  and _____? This latter is a front that hides a deeper _____ to

  be noticed and _____. It produces the _____ of what you really

  want. It marks you as an _____ person. If you want to bring others into genuine friendship,

  it does not _____ the type of friend kind you want to notice and _____ you. It

  goes in the _____ direction. So determine to be _____ and

  _____. Choose to make _____ to reflect who you want others to see. It may

  be awkward to begin with, but _____ produces _____. Choose your

  friends, but choose them _____.

The Big Choice – Choosing Your Husband

Let God do it! As you submit your choices and _____ to Him, He will prompt,

_____ and encourage you all along this journey.

Write down your "Wrong Prayer" ; then think it through._____

_____

_____

Write down your "Right Prayer"; then dwell on it and commit to it. _____

_____

Choose to keep your focus for your special man on who he is as a young man of _____, not on his

handsome _____ and all he does and can do – the things that make him _____.

Discernment lives within _____ as is your divinely guided _____ of being

able to tell what is good as opposed to what is bad. In today's society, overwhelmed with focus on

_____, the eye is often _____ by outward beauty. When you

_____ God – even in your excitement – you are _____.Feelings cannot be

_____ because they are fleeting.

When tendered with time, you will walk in the _____ of your choices, treasuring how your

Heavenly Father is _____ you and _____ for you in such personal ways.

It Is Not Just the Man You Are Choosing

Engagement is the time for preparation. Part of that is in really getting to _____ his family and their

_____. Finish out the following questions:

1. How does he speak_____
2. Is he _____
3. How does he _____
4. Are they _____
5. Does he enjoy _____
6. Is he_____
7. Does he_____
8. Does he _____
9. Does he show_____
10. How do his parents_____
11. Do they _____
12. Is one _____
13. What are their _____

As you watch personality and character patterns, remember that what you see in the home is what you can

_____ to be the _____ in your home. When you marry you do not leave

the _____ back at your parents' home; you _____ it with you. He will

model those _____ and _____ he has lived with.

Your Wedding

This is the most _____ decision of your life other than your choice to become a Christian. Be

certain your inner beauty is prepared and _____ even in a greater way than the outward.

Let what you do be decent and in _____. Be _____ and use good sense. Wisdom says to work _____ your means and don't try to _____ something you are not. Your wedding is not to up-stage the weddings of your friends. Good taste and _____ must over-ride it all.

You Are Now A Wife

God's Word says for a wife to _____ her husband. He is the _____ of the home according to God's Word. You are there to meet _____ needs and he is there to _____ your needs. His prime needs are _____ and _____. Cut all ties with former _____ partners; don't leave this door _____. Period. Allowing _____ to continue will work _____ in a marriage. Submit to his leadership. If you consider yourself to have _____ leadership abilities than he, you must _____ him to be leader even when he struggles.

You as a Mother

The unequaled thrill of that new baby will bring out levels of humanity like no other. Here is where you and your husband must _____ to establish _____ between you so you are able to _____ some degree of sanity. Because the _____ is normally the extender of _____ from the time of birth through the young child's life, she is the one the children _____ on the most for what they need. It is good to be depended upon, but this can lead you to _____ on them for your _____. You must train both your children and your _____. Your children must be told to go to their _____. Your husband may need to be brought to _____ as to how to _____ to his children. Both you and your husband are to establish the _____ of your home and what you _____ it to be as a Christ-centered _____ for the family. The _____ is where they learn what _____ Christianity really is.

Declaration

> "Knowing my husband and I are a powerhouse in the Kingdom of God, I choose to be relentless in holding onto godly values in establishing our Christian home. I will be bold in training up my children in the way they should go. I will boldly show the love of Jesus for each family member, knowing God will bless it. I will then see the reward of our children and their children serving their Lord and living righteously. This is my greatest reward as a mother, and I look forward to it."

7th Foundation – Your Power Sources

THE BLOOD OF JESUS – THE NAME OF JESUS – THE WORD OF GOD

"If you want to experience Jesus Christ and His power, you must get up from where you are and start moving in His direction" – Rick Renner

You need power because the enemy is constantly trying to bring you down so you will become discouraged, give up, and give in. God has given you _____ over the _____ with three _____ satan and all his domain _____ contend with.   Declaring these to the enemy causes him to stop _____. His knees are _____ and he furiously _____ in fear.

The Blood of Jesus

As you read through my encounter as a young boy with the power of satan, I trust you realized how critical it is to teach your children from a very young age the power in their tongue over all the enemy's pressures. By knowing this, my sister's life was saved and I was spared life in prison or even death.

Jesus' Blood shed for you as He was crucified on the cross is a _____ never to be without in your life. It is _____ not only to your salvation, but to _____ in _____ throughout every area of your life.

Unlike the liberal church not wanting to be "offensive", we must never _____ from the Bible what the _____ might find to be "gross" in order to _____ and _____ what we don't like to look at.   God established "the life is in the blood" as His divine and _____ _____ to be life-giving.   Without it, there can be no _____life. Without it there can be no _____life.

Understanding Blood Sacrifices

Read Leviticus chapters 1-7.

This process was the way God – prior to salvation through _____ shedding His _____ on the cross – established for His people to secure _____ for sins.

The shedding of blood was always, still is, and always _____ _____ the element through which _____ is provided. **Read Matthew 26:28.**

The difference from the Old Testament – pre-Jesus Christ – way is that Jesus did it _____ and for all time.   Absolutely nothing else can _____anything to this sacrifice for completeness.

So There is Power in the Blood of Jesus!

It is through the shedding of His _____ as He was crucified that we have _____ of sin. Coming to Him for your initial born-again experience does not take care of sin _____ from that point on. You have that privilege of going to Him again and again as you sense the need for _____ and _____.

Jesus' Blood is Power Over Satan and his Demons

Satan Cannot Cross the Blood Line

As a believer you have the _____ to use the power in the Blood of Jesus against _____ and all his _____. Secure this gem of understanding in your spirit and be confident in it as you read Leviticus 17:11.

The power of life and death is in your tongue. One of your scriptures to memorize is Proverbs. 18:21.

The death angel described in Exodus 11 and 12 could not enter the homes of those where the doorposts were painted with blood. God protected His people with His Blood and the enemy COULD NOT go past that Blood line.

God has set the Blood of His chosen Lamb as a _____ over which the enemy in no way can _____. You, a believer, are washed in the Blood of the Lamb and satan _____ touch you in any way – that is, except by your _____.

The blood is the payment for sin

Write it down Hebrews 9:22:_____

_____

_____

Remission is _____ for something. Jesus purchased your salvation through the shedding of His

_____ on the cross. We can do nothing beyond what has been done by Jesus to

_____ it or _____ Him back in some way. He desires your love, but that is

not to pay back; it is the _____ He wants to have with you.

The Blood

- ✓ Is for Our Redemption: See Ephesians 1:7

- ✓ Is Atonement for our Sins: See Romans 3:25

- ✓ Justifies Us: See Romans 5:9

For a More Thorough Understanding:

Read and study Hebrews 9:11-27. It firmly sets in place the subject of where the power in the Blood comes from.

The Name of Jesus

This is your family name. The blood in your system is the true essence of _____ you REALLY are.

Because, at the time of your _____ you became a "child of God" – you were

_____ _____ - you are a member of the _____ of God.

You own the _____ and right to use your "family name" as a sign of your

_____ - who you are in Christ. Because Jesus lives in you, all _____ of evil have

to _____ _____ when you declare whose authority you _____ in.

Memorize:

- ➤ *"God exalted Him to the highest place and gave Him the name that is above every name, that at the name of Jesus every knee should bow, in heaven and on earth and under the earth, and every tongue confess that Jesus Christ is Lord, to the glory of God the Father." Philippians 2:9-11*

When you pray, be comfortable speaking "in Jesus' name". The power in that name is bombastic. Your words are

_____ of power against the enemy. Your power over the enemy is

_____ through your spoken word in the name of Jesus.

Because of Jesus' name, you have immediate and _____ access to the throne of God. You don't have to go through a chain of command or channels of _____ to get permission. He is right _____ right _____ for you.

THE NAME OF JESUS IS:

(Write out the following scriptures)

- **Relational: Matthew 18:20 -** _____

  _____

  _____

- **Power: John 16:23 -** _____

  _____

  _____

- **Provisional: John 16:24 -** _____

  _____

  _____

- **Complete: Colossians 3:17 -** _____

  _____

  _____

- **Most Supreme: Hebrews 1:4** _____

  _____

  _____

- **Everlasting: Revelation 3:5 -** _____

  _____

  _____

- **The Word of God: Revelation 19:13: -** _____

  _____

  _____

The Word of God

This is the third power source you have at your disposal. It is like the others: _____

_____ _____ _____

_____ _____.

Memorize:

> ➢ *"For the Word of God is living and active, sharper than any double-edged sword, it penetrates even to dividing soul and spirit, joints and marrow; it judges the thoughts and attitudes of the heart." Hebrews 4:12*

Jesus, when He was subjecting Himself to temptation, used the Word _____ satan. In each temptation He used the Word as _____ against the enemy.

Satan will try to use the Word of God against you to _____ you. He will always take it out of

_____ . Satan cannot tell the _____ .

When you speak the Word, satan _____ be successful in coming against what you say.

Memorize:

> ➢ *"Submit yourselves, then, to God. Resist the devil, and he will flee from you." James 4:7*

Whatever you use from the Word of God is _____ against satan. Satan cannot read your thoughts. You must speak out loud. Your words must be thrust forth into the _____ because that is satan's _____ . Anything _____ his air waves is instantly recognized.

Each verse of scripture is a _____ arrow in your arsenal against the enemy.

Write Psalm 119:11 -_____

_____

_____

What is inside you _____ come out; what is _____ inside is not powerful and effectual _____ the enemy.

As you read your Bible and a particularly meaningful scripture verse reaches out to you, _____ that one and put it in your collection to _____ . Commit them to memory. Hide them in your heart.

These are your swords against the attacks of the enemy. You have built a power house within you against satan and his army.

This powerhouse of deposits in your _____ is there for you to be _____ in your knowing what is truth and then giving you the _____ your footsteps are on _____ foundations. They guide you in the _____ of Christ-like living and your _____ integrity. You will not waiver and you will live in _____ and contentment as a result of your right _____ and resultant actions.

Declaration

"Father, I choose to use the power sources You have given me to use. Thank You for Your Word, Your Blood, and Your Name. I choose to walk in my authority over the enemy and all his forces, knowing he cannot prevail against the weapons You have given."

8th Foundation – Knowledge, Understanding, and Wisdom

KNOW YOUR ENEMY

As in any circumstance when you are coming up against an oppressor, you must be equipped for the battlefield so you are always the victor and not the victim. If it were improper to give attention to satan in order to know his schemes, God would never have prepared you by exposing him. Your thorough understanding of who is opposing you is preparation for being a consistent _____.

Some people take the position that talking about satan is giving him undue attention and taking time away from talking about God. **Rather than giving satan and his demons undue attention, you are _____ him for all he is there to do _____ you, the child of God.**

There is absolutely no reason to fear _____ and _____ about satan and his army. Expanding your knowledge base regarding satan is _____. You have been given _____ through the Holy Spirit who lives in you to overcome and _____ the enemy _____ time he come against you.

Read and digest right now 1 Peter 5:8 & 9
You can see one of his tactics is to bring _____. All you have to do each time is to resist him in the name of Jesus. He has to back off, go away, crumble, _____.
Recite James 4:7. You have already memorized it.

Satan's Two Fold Purpose
First: His chief purpose is to _____

_____

Second: His ongoing purpose is _____

The wonderful victorious life you walked into at the time of your salvation is also a life of _____ the evil one as he chooses to _____ every child of God.

The encouraging truth in the whole process of understanding is that the enemy has _____, no matter what, and you are _____ in _____ situation. The only way satan can have any _____ is that you come into _____ with what he is trying to do to bring you down.

Ways Satan Uses To Bring You Down

1. **Deception**

    Deception is the umbrella under which all sin is committed!!

    > # Deception is the thinking that doing something different from what is right will produce a greater, more rewarding and beneficial outcome.

    Deception Happens This Way:

    *   Satan brings you_____

    *   You dwell _____

    *   Temptation_____

    *   You _____

    Every sin is introduced through _____ means. It is your _____.

    Let's consider these:

    *   The picture, imagination, item: _____did it come from?

    *   It is something you _____ you would like to _____ or like to _____.

    Right here you must immediately _____ what is taking place and use your _____ over satan and what he is _____ to get you into.

    Right now is where you make your _____: to _____ to the temptation or to _____ the devil and tell him to _____ in Jesus' name!! Cover your mind with the _____ of Jesus and then choose to _____ on things that are good and pure.

3. Lies

Since satan is the father of lies, he can speak _____ but lies. He will plant lies into your mind and make you think they are your thoughts.

Write down right now some lies he tries to trap you with:_____

_____

_____

_____

Now, using your authority against satan, tell him whose you are; resist those lies; tell him to flee.

4. Temptation

He will show you something attractive to you, something you would like to have or even something great you have not even thought of yet. If you don't _____ right now and call his _____, you will walk out the _____ desires and fulfill satan's trickery right here. The key to not yielding to temptation is to _____ _____ where the thought (the voice) is coming from and _____ it immediately. Here is what you say: "I am committed to God. Satan, I resist you and you have to flee". Say it out loud and mean it.

5. Discouragement

Courage is a life character.   Read Deuteronomy 31:6. The purpose of satan in bringing discouragement is to _____ what God has already spoken and to bring _____ to you.

6. Fear

Fear is the direct antithesis (opposite) of faith and trust. Your thoughts will always take you to where you don't want to go if you _____ to fear. God said, "I have not given you a spirit of fear, but of _____, _____, and a _____ mind" 2 Timothy 1:7. KJV Satan comes hard in this area because fear can affect our _____ with God by bringing _____. Make a choice right now to not succumb to fear in any _____, _____, or form.

7. Worry

Worry is walking in the _____ that what your Heavenly Father has in place for you actually will not be there as He has _____. Through worry, satan can keep you from experiencing God's _____ for you and keep you from being a victorious-life _____ before others. Worry defies the _____ of God in your life.

8. **Doubt**

   In order to not yield to doubt, you have to _____ that your belief in God will not be
   wavering or _____. Read Hebrews 10:23. The key word here is _____
   _____. Often, doubt begins to be considered when a respected person who is not a
   believer has opposing opinions regarding God's _____, His _____, and
   His _____. You are to bring them to the truth, not consider
   _____it.

9. **Shame**

   Satan will bring up your past, causing you to _____ you are fatally
   _____ and that _____ can change that.   First off, he is a liar. He
   CANNOT speak the _____. He wants to bring you _____ from walking in
   God's _____ and _____ for you. Read Isaiah 43:25.
   Be encouraged that your shame is entirely _____ beyond the possibility of being
   _____.

10. **Unbelief**

    Choosing to not believe something about the great life of joy as a child of God severly
    _____ going forward.   Unbelief builds a foundation to such an extent that your belief
    in _____ is being _____ and your faith is being undermined with
    _____ ideas.   Read 1 Cor. 2:14 Determine to _____ unbelief right now.
    Declare, "Whatever God says, even though it may seem _____ far out, it is truth and I believe it."

These are just a few of the areas satan uses to keep you from growing in your faith and maturing as a child of God.

Right now ask the Lord and the Holy Spirit to quicken your mind to recognize something going on that is

_____ to your spirit. Give the Holy Spirit _____ to deal with that in you

even when you would rather not go there. This process will keep any issues from _____ into

_____ in your life. Nip it in the bud!

The Nature of God - The Nature of Satan

Everything God is – satan is the opposite!!

As you consider the characteristics in the chart in your book, you will be quickened to recognize the ungodly nature of feelings you deal with. Knowing this principle will help you to move out of the enemy's _____ and into God's _____ principles; they are always best.

KNOW YOUR ENEMY'S TACTICS

- He works in your _____, most _____ areas

- Because you are firm in your "NO" _____ _____, he does not stop.

- The pictures and ideas _____

- He will convince you that _____

  _____

- He makes you _____

- He will not_____

- He works to _____

In the story of David, you could relate to the tactics of the enemy. But, be encouraged. God is always there to _____ and will do that for any _____ heart. However, forgiveness never absolves the _____ for the _____ of the sin.

The example in David's life is a classic scene of SHAME-FEAR-CONTROL. It is a damning cycle most everyone – if not everyone – walks in _____ or _____ times. The _____ of David's sin caused him to _____ that he would be _____. So he took _____ to keep that from happening. You can see here deception for what it really is.

Lesser, More Ordinary Temptations

The Lie: This is, I believe, the first sin a little child commits. It continues through the lives of many people as not too serious. It is how satan get his "fatherhood" nature injected into each life.

A breach of _____ is very difficult to mend; it takes a very long time for _____ to be _____. By applying the reality of _____ as a guard to any thought, you can keep yourself in _____, protecting you from walking ahead into that _____ spiral satan tempts you with. The key is to _____

_____.

Time for You To Think

Name some other temptations you face from time to time. BE real. Be honest with yourself. This is your book and not open to the eyes of anyone else.

_____   _____

_____   _____

_____   _____

Then, make your choice to never go there. Make them in advance. If you wait until you are in the midst of a _____ situation to make the right choice, you are weak and vulnerable and often _____, thus making the _____ choice under the _____ of the moment.

God's enabling grace is with you at all times. One of the scriptures identified for you to memorize is Isaiah 41:10. Refresh your mind on this right now. Get it into your heart. Take advantage of God's strength and power in your life. You will be an _____.

When the enemy is bombarding you with _____, recall 1 John 4:4 which says: _____ _____

You never need to be _____ because there is enough power at work in you to resist _____ _____ coming against you, no matter how strong.

Scriptures Satan Hates

Refer to these in your book. Have them for quick reference. Establish them in your heart. They are for your overcoming. Operate in that mighty force and power your Heavenly Father has placed _____ you. Use the _____ of God against satan and his forces. Never back down and show _____. You will be the _____ every time.

Declaration

"Father, right now I choose to be the overcomer You desire me to be so I can be all that I desire to be for You. I ask You, Holy Spirit, to help me recognize the enemy's invasion in my mind and then for the instant recognition. I choose to resist every time and be victorious in the battle against satan."

9th Foundation – Take Charge

THOUGHTS, THOUGHTS, THOUGHTS

You CANNOT be transformed except by the _____ of your _____.

Satan has a hay-day with what _____ causes to be _____ in your mind.   You have the ability

to - _____ or _____ his input. If you are like most people, you struggle

with your _____ life.

**Unless your thinking is renewed
and comes under the Lordship of Christ,
your transformation is not possible.
It is the rock-solid fact.**

Just as your computer hard drive needs to be occasionally de-fragmented, so does your mind. Let's get it renewed

so your whole life process can be transformed. The devil and his forces are _____ _____ that

hate you. They are seeking to _____ you. He wants access to your life; and if you don't keep the

door _____, he will get in.

Ephesians 6:12

You have already committed this verse to memory, or you soon will be.

The greatest protection you have in winning the battles against the forces in this verse is your mind dominated by

_____ _____.   The Word will give you _____ and

protection, bringing you freedom from _____ and other _____.

But, you say, my thoughts are just there! Yes, that seems to be true. So here are the steps to help you take

charge.

- Instantly _____identify the new thought.
- Is it _____ or is it of God and something _____ to think on?
- If temptation, speak God's Word: (Write it down):_____

- If it is God, _____

- The more you check your _____, the more _____ you will be in knowing the _____ of each one coming to you.

    Memorize
    - ➢ *"Do not be deceived: God cannot be mocked. A man reaps what he sows."* **Galatians 6:7**

If you think you are strong enough to play around with some enticing thing for a little while and then take charge and _____ satan later because God is merciful, you are right in the _____ where the enemy wants you. You are ripe for being overcome and _____ the battle.

God is always open for repentance, but _____ presume on His _____; that is dangerous living and the consequences are _____.

You must _____ your mind. You must _____ your thoughts. You must recognize _____ thoughts not in line with His _____, His _____, or His _____.

It is not enough to just _____ and deny those thoughts; nor is it enough to just _____ them out. You must create new _____ thoughts to replace the lies you have bought into. So, go ahead and make this declaration right now:

"Lord, I want my mind renewed so I can be transformed throughout all my ways so I can live the kind of life pleasing to you. I choose to do what it takes because I want to be free to be all You have destined for me."

Thought Habits

There are patterns of thought and thought habits people live with as protective boundaries. Many of these are to keep us from being _____. Others are to protect others from knowing who we _____ are deep down inside. They are developed from _____ experiences, often from very early in _____ and throughout life. As a result, we have chosen to protect ourselves by determining to keep _____ the _____ wounds others have caused. So we create _____ ways to deal with the _____ by forming _____ to help us live with it.

> # Thoughts release permission or refusal.
> # Choice takes control over thoughts.

God desires for us to be free from _____ and _____, but until we _____ our hurts and give them to Him, they _____ go away. They keep us in _____ so we do not come into a life of complete _____ in our emotions and feelings.   Our spirit stays _____ and our heart stays _____.

You could see in Micah's life how something he kept secret from very early in life kept him from moving forward until it was brought to Jesus for healing.

SOME MAJOR THOUGHT TRAPS FOR MOST PEOPLE

✓ **Fear**

Are you a person who lives in fear of something? Someone? If you think that fear is not a bad thing, your _____ is wrong. Throughout God's Word we are continually reminded to fear not; do not _____; do not be _____. Fear keeps you from being your _____ self.

✓ **Worry**

Worry is wasted imagination. Worry _____ faith. You can never accomplish any _____ results by worrying. To overcome worry, you must choose – make a _____ - directing your mind to _____ on the protection and _____ of your Heavenly Father. You must determine to walk in _____, not _____.   Worry is like a security blanket protecting fear and holding it in place.

Declaration

"Father, in Jesus' name, I choose from this time on to live a life of faith. I choose to trust You in all things, knowing You are taking care of me in everything. Satan, you can no longer enter my mind giving me worried thoughts. I resist you, and you have to flee. Amen."

✓ **Anger**

Anger, as an emotion, is both bad and good. Anger comes from a deeper root - _____.
Uncontrolled anger manifests itself in _____. When a person gives in to the _____ of anger and lets it have its way, this is precisely what the enemy is wanting His purpose is three-fold: to _____, _____, and _____.
Anger is good only when you are angry at _____. Your angry demeanor is seen by people and they choose to not approach you because of your _____ of control.

✓ **UNWORTHINESS**

The feeling no value, no _____, no significance and no _____ to have a _____. Unworthiness brings _____, especially as it relates to your Heavenly _____. It is God who made you _____ through the cross of Christ and the _____ shed on that cross for you. God makes only things of _____, _____, _____, and _____ with a unique place for His special design – that is you!!!

✓ **REJECTION**

Rejection makes you feel unwanted, not included, set-aside, un-chosen, and avoided. The resident attitude of rejection also attacks your _____. Being set aside and seeing others moved into your desired place wrestles with your _____. Feelings of rejection is where many people give satan place. You give him _____ _____ by agreeing that you are not worthy of being chosen.   If he can bring you down into discouragement because of _____ of rejection, he has you right where he _____ you.

✓ Your strength and confidence is always in the Word of the Lord because it is the truth. It over-powers the lie every time.

  ➢ "...*I will never leave you or forsake you.*" Heb. 13:5

These more common thought habits- fear, worry, anger, unworthiness, and rejection – are the more prominent thread is the fabric of _____ satan weaves for us to _____ by. When you agree to these thought habits, you are giving him _____ _____ to do his work. You have developed _____ thought patterns to live by. Because of them, you have made judgments and _____ in order to _____ who satan says you are and, also, to _____ yourself from being _____.

Are you living by any of the thought pattern examples giving in your book? Right now, ask the Holy Spirit to reveal to you what beliefs you have bought into that are not godly. Be truthful. Be real with yourself. Go ahead and write them down right here:_____

_____

_____

_____

_____

Take charge right now. Finish the following statements. Review them daily until your spirit is causing you to live in truth.

- ✓ I choose to obey_____

  _____

- ✓ Realizing worry is _____

  _____

- ✓ When I sense_____

  _____

- ✓ Understanding the manner_____

  _____

  _____

- ✓ My approval by others _____

  _____

  _____

Each of the previous godly beliefs brings truth to the _____ of the ungodly belief. The truth is always _____ than the lie. This is the process of renewing your mind so you can be _____. Transformation can only come through the _____. What is not changed and re-programmed there will not _____ in the final product.

Get Complete Healing – Take Charge

Most, if not all, people are living with some degree of un-forgiveness. _____ keeps us from humbling ourselves before another person. _____ causes us to fear exposure and retaliation. So we take _____ to protect what we are hiding. Until you are willing to _____ yourself in every detail of your life, you will _____ get your _____ so you can walk in complete _____.

Normally, a person cannot accomplish this without help from another person because it is difficult to see ourselves realistically and truthfully. Professionally trained and qualified counselors guided by the Holy Spirit are those to seek out for your healing.

So, I say all that to tell you to TAKE CHARGE and get help! Put aside those thoughts you struggle with. Satan will bombard you with submission and pride. But whom do you really want to serve and be free?

The point where you can't come to grips with your struggles is where you stop growing

---

Forgiveness

Forgiveness is the vehicle through which most all healing is derived. Un-forgiveness will keep you from _____ into the fullness of your _____. Forgiveness does not happen when _____, _____, and qualifications are specified. Forgiveness is a _____, not a feeling. Forgiveness is _____ in action. Forgiveness does not require _____.

What you don't forgive, you are bound to relive.

If it were not for forgiveness, you would not be a Christian! Jesus has told us that if we do not forgive we _____ be forgiven. There are no _____ to forgiveness. Think of those people right now you need to forgive and get going. Don't hold back. Get your complete freedom in process. Use this prayer as a guide to help you.

> **Lord Jesus, I choose right now to live a life of forgiveness. Therefore, I forgive _____ for anything done to me and for not being to me what I needed. I ask You, Heavenly Father, to bless them in Your chosen ways which are far greater than I can even imagine. Now I ask You to forgive me, Lord, for my reluctance, and I receive Your forgiveness. Amen**

Starting now, ask the Holy Spirit to bring others to your mind who you need to forgive.

Now You Are Ready

Ready to move into the second part of Romans 12:2: *". . . Then you will be able to test and approve what God's will is – His good, pleasing and perfect will."*

With a unclear and uncertain mind full of bunches of "stuff" going on that overshadows your ability to _____ the voice of God and think _____ in what He is saying, you are not able to _____ any direction God is _____ to bring you.

All children of God have this great passion to find what God's _____ and _____ are for them. It is a growing process. God directs you in His ways _____ upon _____ and _____ upon _____. As you move in _____, not becoming impatient, He sees you as _____ to handle more with greater _____ and _____. Your God-given destiny _____ this way.

I Want It My Way:

Too often we ask God to help us to get where _____ want to go: we want God control our lives _____ making us yield to Him the goals we have already set in place. Correct this tendency by:

1. Turning over_____

2. Do what you _____

3. Listen_____

Once you have come to the place of being renewed and not _____ by _____ and glamorous stories, you are _____ enough in your sure footing that you can really hear and _____ your Heavenly Father's _____. You are comfortable with what He says and are able to be _____ in walking into the plans to be uncovered _____ the way.

YOUR PURPOSE CALL: Right here you must understand there is a difference between the "anointing "and the "appointing". Caution must be exercised so you do not move ahead of God's timing.

> # There is a difference in WHAT you are called to do and WHEN you are called to go.

Most often the call is given as a _____ for you to make thorough _____ to be ready when He gives _____ to step into action of your purpose and plan.

When you drive to an unknown destination, you turn on your GPS and depend on each direction it gives, being told of each move just prior to doing it. When you follow God's guidance, you know you are where God _____ wants you, whether you are _____ or _____ in one place. He has a purpose in _____ you where you are right now.

Because you are moving into being transformed, your _____ and your _____ are in the proper place to _____ Go and be _____ with what you hear.

Declaration

"Father, I choose to be at peace with what I hear You say to me. I choose to be content and to receive Your purposes and plans. I choose to be diligent in preparing myself to be ready when any new direction is given. I choose to be patient through the process. Then, I choose to be obedient and move as You order my steps."

10th Foundation – Unfailing Mentor

THE HOLY SPIRIT AND YOU

The Holy Spirit – the complete foundation and working out of your faith as a child of God is incomplete without the intimate involvement of the Holy Spirit. He – notice, I said "He" – is _____ to God and Jesus as the _____ part of the God-head, the Trinity.

Christian

The Christian has been drawn by the _____ _____. For one to say he is a Christian because he simply _____ about Christianity does not make him a _____. Then, too, to say he is a Christian but is not _____ with the Holy Spirit speaks of a _____ of understanding of who the Holy Spirit is. You cannot be a Christian _____ the work of the Holy Spirit because it is He who _____ you to repentance.

When you are addressing God, you are including _____ _____ parts of the trinity. When you pray to _____, it is all three. (Three in one) When you speak to the Father, you are calling to His unique _____ and quality within the element of the trinity – such things as relate to his _____ nature. He oversees, provides, and _____ you. When you speak to Jesus, you relate to His nature as _____, _____, and brother with whom you are an equal heir. When you speak of the Holy Spirit, you relate to Him as _____, _____, and _____.

When you call on God, you are bringing together all the _____ of the combined trinity. Most people have a real _____ in their understanding of the Holy Spirit. He longs for you, _____ about you, desires to be _____ to you, and wants to _____ Himself to you. Even Jesus _____ the Holy Spirit. He _____ on the Holy Spirit during His earthly ministry. He . . . .

- was_____ by the Holy Spirit (Luke 1:35)
- was_____ by the Holy Spirit (Matthew 3:16)
- was_____ (Matthew 4:1)
- _____ by the power of the Holy Spirit (Acts 10:38)

- _____ by the power of the Holy Spirit (Matt.12:28)
- Was _____ from the dead (Romans 8:11)
- Was _____ (Eph 1: 19, 20)

> **Communion with the Holy Spirit is the launching pad for a life of supernatural power and consistency.**

Just Who Is The Holy Spirit?

Yes, you read it right. Not _____ is the Holy Spirit. He is the _____ PERSON of the trinity. He is not an _____, or object or _____ animation. Jesus took care of you and provided for you when He left. Read John 14:16-18. And John 14:26

An advocate is one who pleads the _____ of another – one who _____ or maintains a cause. Jesus is the _____, the _____, and the _____. So His Spirit – the Spirit of Truth – is what He left us to _____ in after He went to be with His Father. The Holy Spirit empowers you to _____ the cause of Christ, in other words, to live _____ as a child of God. The Holy Spirit is here to _____ Christ's literal _____ living with you.   Just as Jesus did nothing other than what the Father had for Him to do, the Holy Spirit is in _____ for specifically that same _____ as it relates to Jesus and all He _____ for you. Jesus lived only to be _____ to His Father, to _____ and maintain the cause of all the Father had _____ in His love for _____ peoples. So the Holy Spirit is now living here – living in _____ as a Child of God – to maintain the cause of the _____ life here on earth.

> ➤ *"Do you not know that your bodies are temples of the Holy Spirit, who is in you, whom you have received from God? You are not your own."* **1 Corinthians 6:19**

When Did He Start to Live in Me?
At the time you came to receive Jesus as your Savior, the Holy Spirit _____ in and took residence.

What Will He Do for Me?

- **He will help you.**

  Read John 15:26 NKJ Just as Jesus reflected the _____, the Holy Spirit has the same _____ to Jesus. He is in you to help you in _____. You can depend on Him, also, to lead you and give you deeper _____ and

  _____.

- **He will teach you.**

  Read John 14:25, 26. Then read Nehemiah 9:20.

  As a child of God, you are _____ to receive the truth, to _____ the truth, and to _____ in it. As you read your Bible, He will fill in your _____ of understanding by _____ to you deeper _____ of what you are reading about. No revelation counter to what God is saying can _____ come from the Holy Spirit. Read 1 John 2:27

- **He will guide you.**

  Read John 16:13. When you are tempted in some area, the Holy Spirit speaks up _____, _____ you as you move out of the truth. Conviction is a good reminder because it brings you to _____. Condemnation brings on _____ and is not the purpose of the Holy Spirit. The Holy Spirit sees what you _____ see, _____ what you don't know, and _____ the best direction for you. It is essential to _____ on Him to lead you.

> *"Now, therefore, there is no condemnation to those who are in Christ Jesus."* **Romans 8:1**

Even back in the Old Testament, Isaiah prophesies concerning Jesus and the Holy Spirit's _____ in His life. See Isaiah 11:2. You can see that the Father _____ His Son with a companion. You see in it the character qualities of the Holy Spirit.

- ✓ Spirit of _____
- ✓ Spirit of _____
- ✓ Spirit of _____
- ✓ Spirit of _____
- ✓ Spirit of _____
- ✓ Spirit of _____

And There Is More: The Three Baptisms

1. **The baptism of repentance**

    See Acts 19:4 and Acts 2:38

2. **The baptism in water**

    See Colossians 2:12 and 1 Peter 3:21. Also Jesus' baptism in Matthew 3:13-16

3. **The baptism of the Holy Spirit and fire**

    See Acts 2:38 – a key verse

Read the Story in Acts Chapter 2

Each one in the crowd heard in their own _____ with all the inflections and

characteristic flavors what was being said by these _____, not highly educated folks. They

realized that no way could this have taken place in the _____; it was beyond the shadow of a

doubt _____!

Those who were speaking in tongues (_____, _____ language) had no

_____ of any language different from their own native tongue. It was translated by the

Holy Spirit into the _____ of the crowd in order for each one to understand the

_____ of the _____ of Christ in his own _____ dialect.

What happened here was a demonstration of the _____ of the _____

_____ with the evidence of speaking in _____.

This Same Baptism is for You Today

You may ask, "How do I receive it?" **Just ask!!**

See Luke 11:13 - this is your example. You receive it _____ you ask. It is the same principle as asking

for salvation. You instantly _____ it. In either circumstance, not all the _____

show up in an instant. But – in _____ - you walk out what you have received. You may not break out in

your heavenly _____ yet. But by the truth of God's Word, you know that what you have asked for

has been _____ to you.

You cannot judge the truth by _____ - you judge the truth by the _____ of God only.

Now, take advantage of this "power" you never had before in the same _____. Begin to depend on

the Holy Spirit to be your _____, your _____, your _____, your

_____ and many other things to _____ you with.

He wants to protect you. Be alert to His quiet prompting; don't just pass it off as something that "just popped into your mind." Trust what He is saying. Then greater _____ comes.

For you to pray: At this time, go to your book and read aloud the prayer.

The Outward Manifestation – Speaking in Tongues

See Acts 19:6. The lack of immediate speaking in an unknown tongue is no indication of your not _____ this wonderful gift.   You have received it, or God's Word would not be _____. The word says the baptism in the Holy Spirit is received by _____. Now you must _____ that you have _____ and walk in _____ that it is actual.

Be sure your emphasis of your desire is not on the _____ of the gift, but on receiving the _____ of the Holy Spirit in ALL HIS FULLNESS. The manifestation may come _____ through times in prayer.   The "full flow" of your _____ language may not happen all at once. There is usually a "filling-in" developmental process over _____ as the language becomes free, _____, and without hesitation.

It is not _____ on you. Yielding to the Holy Spirit must be your _____, trusting Him _____.

A More Complete Look at What the Bible Says about Speaking in Tongues

- Acts 2:4 -   You can see that it is the Holy Spirit who _____ you the words to speak.
- 1ˢᵗ Corinthians 14:2 KJV - When you speak in tongues, you are talking to God – this is the principle _____.
- 1ˢᵗ Corinthians 14:4 - To edify is to _____ yourself up in your spiritual strength. The more you are built up and strengthened, the more you can _____ and help others.
- 1ˢᵗ Corinthians 14:14, 15 - Understanding what you are saying is not _____ because it is the Holy Spirit praying _____ you.

Speaking in tongues is "praying in the _____". There is cause for praying both in your _____ language and in the language of the _____.

One of the key advantages of praying in tongues is your _____ from satan's involvement. Satan cannot understand your prayer because he is not _____. He may hear, but he cannot understand. In faith you receive all the self-edification you can handle with your present _____ and growth. As you pray in your prayer language and continue the practice of it, what you have been given by God will begin to be _____ as time progresses.

So, exercise your faith. Faith is _____ that what God's Word says is truth. Your wisdom in the Holy Spirit is always more deeply _____ than the natural _____ of others who appear to be _____ knowledgeable than you.

As you make praying in the spirit a practice in your life, you will realize your _____ becoming more firmly _____ as you represent Jesus Christ and His choice purpose for your life.

Your Hard-Core Check up

PART 1: THE NAKED TRUTH

Christian living combined with the works of the flesh and the accepted life patterns of today do not compute. To be blunt right up front; **there are those living in today's society believing they are Christians who really are not.** Until they come into entire subjection to the righteousness of God's Word, they are in place for the most horrid shock of their lives. They have not really lived what they believed in order to enter the Kingdom of God. **This is serious, serious business!**

Let's make certain you understand the works of the flesh and how continuing in them actually disqualifies you from being a Christian. This is a hard truth. The Bible tells us we perish from a lack of knowledge. **Therefore, anyone who reads this has no excuse.**

> ## Is the manner of your living keeping you from walking in the blessings you desire from God for your life?

I want you to see at once, in today's language, this vital area in God's Word:

> [19] Now the works of the flesh are manifest, which are *these;* Adultery, fornication, uncleanness, lasciviousness, [20] idolatry, witchcraft, hatred, variance, emulations, wrath, strife, seditions, heresies, [21] envyings, murders, drunkenness, revellings, and such like: of the which I tell you before, as I have also told *you* in time past, that they which do such things shall not inherit the kingdom of God. [1] Gal. 5:19-21 (NIV)

> ## Two Things God Does Not Tolerate:
> ## Other gods before Him
> ## His people with sin in their lives.

Galatians 5:19-21 specifies the sinful practices as "_____ of the flesh"

This is not about being "perfect" and not _____ making a mistake. It says that if you

_____ to live with any of these _____ in your life as standard,

ongoing practice, you are living _____ the salvation you once thought you chose but really

_____ mean it.

Be careful to not fall into the _____ of satan telling you God _____ your desires and will _____ them because you are sincere, loving, and kind. Deception grows deep here.

Remember, deception is taking the _____ road believing the end results will be more _____ than taking the _____ road.

So, what is required as a child of God to live in righteousness? Deuteronomy 10:12 tells you in a nutshell.

A Closer Look at These Works of the Flesh

I suggest, prior to your continuing, that you read Psalm 34.

- **Adultery-Fornication**

  The greek word "porneia" encompasses sexual activity _____ marriage. Continuing in a life of adultery thinking it is _____ for the Christian is _____ God's Word, His nature, His principles, and His character.

  When a person engages in pornographic writings and pictures, it is committing mental _____. See Matthew 5:28

  Today's culture is promoting the idea that it is alright to live together outside the _____ of marriage so long as "we are living like a married couple" Just be certain you establish your life in _____ area and live it _____ to God's Word; you can't go wrong.

  God's truths do not change according to people's _____ or societal _____ of acceptance.

- **Uncleanness**

  Entertaining unclean thoughts will ultimately produce lewd or unclean actions. When your mind is allowed to dwell _____ on filthy, impure, dirty thoughts, you will come into _____ with them. Satan has a big _____ here when you have given him permission. Today's society has taken on a _____ in these things implying this is alright because it is our nature; that is satan's lie and _____. You don't want to fall into that trap.

- **Lasciviousness**

  This is one who is given over to _____ - primarily excessive consumption of food and unrestricted _____. In God's mind, _____ in food is placed on the same level as _____ sexual practice. All the works of the flesh can be forgiven, but you must acknowledge and take _____ for your sins. Remember, repentance means to do a _____.

- **Idolatry**

  God's two greatest passions:

  1. He will have _____

  2. He will have _____

  Simply put, idolatry is having any other interest, person, or thing that takes the emphasis or your attention and makes it _____ _____ than a _____ with your Heavenly Father. Your interests for pleasure and recreation are _____ for you. However, they must be kept in _____, always yielding them to who you are in Christ and what He _____ for you.

  Check yourself with some questions about your likes, interests, and the intensity of them. Be real with yourself and be true to yourself.

- **Witchcraft**

  The real meaning of this word in the Greek is the word for medicines or drugs that inhibit a person's personality or changes his behavior – that is, mind-altering drugs. Back in history and on into today people hate to be uncomfortable. Flesh would prefer to learn how to _____ than to be _____ and changed. The Holy Spirit desires to reveal the _____ of the problem so He can bring permanent _____. If you are willing to take charge of your flesh and get it out of the way, God will set you _____ from compulsions, addictions, and dependencies as you _____ to _____ on Him. Don't let an "easier way" keep you from eternal fellowship with your Heavenly Father.

- **Strife**

  Strife manifests a _____, self-centered personality completely _____ with itself that is wholly _____ to the desires and ambitions of _____. It is actually where you put your self-wants before what _____ wants for you. He will not get in your _____ but will let you choose your own.

- **Seditions**

  Are you one who tends to resist and defy authority? If so, you need to consider carefully the Greek meaning that indicates "separation" and "rebellion". The very structure God has established to give you care and _____ becomes the object of _____. If you see yourself rising up _____ an authority in your life, take charge of your attitude and bring it into _____, not allowing this _____ _____ to cause you to step away from your God-destined covering.

- **Heresies**

  The Greek word refers mostly to a division, faction, or an unauthorized group. The flesh loves to believe it is _____, more _____, more qualified, and with deeper _____ than anyone else. You are part of the WHOLE BODY OF CHRIST. No one is even given a revelation or truth so special that it is _____ for a _____-_____ group. Never let the flesh make you think you are a member of a higher _____ class. You will be able to live and _____ as a true child of God and receive the _____ and honor from _____ and others according to the _____ He has given you for the whole body

- **Envyings**

  When someone is envious, it becomes a deep-seated grudge over what someone else has that he aches to have for himself. Your resentfulness of another's _____ will eat at your spirit to the point you will become _____ with how you can _____ that for _____. If you see yourself settling into envy over what someone else is doing, their position, what they have or who they circulate with, call on the Holy Spirit's help to jolt you into _____ of the place and _____ God has for you. Sow _____, _____, _____, _____ and _____ to those people. What you _____ you will _____!!

- **Drunkenness**

  With a mind altered by excessive alcohol consumption, a person _____ think _____. He submits himself to a base desire that surfaces from a _____ spirit that wants to take control and destroy his _____. Satan loves to get the door open a crack so he can _____ it wide open. When our minds are _____ in this way, it leads to works of the _____.

- **Revellings**

    This word describes a person who has to live in un-ending exciting goings-on. Exciting activity and expression all the time – to the extreme.   When a person becomes engaged overwhelmingly in such a life style, he loses _____ as well as good common sense. The "if it feels good, do it" mentality has _____ up with him. He is trapped and now a _____ to seemingly impossible responsibility in order to just _____ and maintain. If this is you, ask yourself several questions:

    - Was all this_____
    - Was it _____
    - Did it have _____
    - Am I _____
    - Could I have_____

    Think of the life-betterment activities of _____ and fulfillment such as developing _____ with other Christian friends.   Look around you and choose some things to make your life more _____ and meaningful for you to enjoy; more importantly, making life more rewarding for _____ around you. You will begin to live with the _____ of your dreams. You will now be equipped to walk into what God can _____ you with.

The Shocking Challenge

As this chapter began, you were told – warned – that living a lifestyle of continuing in such practices put you in _____ of the _____ of what salvation provided for you – your _____ in the kingdom of God. This is very _____ and you must take it very _____. Ask yourself:

- ✓ Am I _____
- ✓ Are any of _____

    _____

Then give the Holy Spirit _____ and be ready to have your spiritual eyes

_____ to see areas you must submit to the _____ of Jesus. Go ahead and

repent so you do not get thrown off guard in your _____ walk. The enemy will get angry and

_____. The good news is that you have the _____ to immediately

overcome his aggression and to tell him to _____.

Confession

"Father, in the name of Jesus, I come to You right now. I am sorry for the ways I have been allowing sinful practices to dominate parts of my life. I choose to not be this way. I repent of _____ (fill in the blank with areas you are confessing). I desire and choose to live a life pleasing to You. I ask You, Holy Spirit, to help me and I give You permission to bring to my mind whatever needs to be brought to the cross. I love You, Father, and am excited about my inheritance of Your Kingdom. Amen."

Your Hard-Core Check up

PART 2: THE FRUIT OF THE SPIRIT

Now, you will be exposed to the characteristic qualities of genuine Christian character and personality.
These are determined as the "fruit" of the Spirit, that word being plural in form.

READ: Galatians 5:22-25

There are eight specified fruit in this collection. Go ahead right now and become a fruit inspector. You will be able
to determine the condition of the "Fruit of the Spirit" in your life. Be ready to change because this fruit is
_____ from that which we eat.

- **Love**

  The expression of love spoken here is from the Greek word *agape.* This is the most in-depth word for
  _____ of the _____ used in the New Testament times. It depicts the
  love of _____; there is no _____. Agape love is so huge that it is
  _____ - it looks beyond and beneath any reason for being
  _____, surpassing all that and bringing into place the genuine
  _____ of agape. It expects _____ in return. This will
  _____ from you and others will be drawn to you because of it.

- **Joy**

  The God kind of joy is _____. It does not change because of circumstances.
  Happiness is affected by _____ and changing situations. Joy is rooted deeply in the
  _____ of the child of God. It is rooted in God's grace and it is frequently realized in
  the _____ times. It flourishes when you are living through tough,
  _____ situations – when you are facing a seemingly impossible mountain in your life.
  This joy is your rest, knowing all _____ work together for the _____ of
  those who are in Christ Jesus.

- **Peace**

  The contentment oozes from your spirit, letting others see you are not overtaken by the issues at hand.

  Your soul is _____. It is _____. It is

  _____. It is _____. It is _____.

- **Longsuffering**

  Tolerant, controlled waiting, restraint. Longsuffering could be explained as long-allowance where

  _____ doesn't come in and ruin the perceived _____ down the road.

- **Gentleness**

  Gentleness wins in any relationship, especially with those of a tender spirit.   This fruit of the Spirit

  manifests a _____ _____ with you. Gentleness is the caring approach

  with a soft manner that will allow others to be _____ to you and to _____ what

  you have for them. It radiates your _____ care and _____ for

  them, no matter how they respond to you at first.

- **Goodness:**

  Your personal goodness is secured in your relationship with Jesus. In the Greek, it has the sense of being

  good to _____. Can you help someone else become more self-sufficient and less

  _____? When someone is down for a period, can you step in and

  _____ a service during that time?

- **Faith**

  This means one who is steady, dedicated, and can be depended on. Here you can see the

  _____ of God Himself and see it as His established _____. Can you

  always be depended on to be where you have _____ to be and perform what you

  have _____ to perform?   Being _____ is the fruit of the Spirit

  showing the _____ of your commitment to Christ.

- **Meekness**

  Meekness is not weakness. Meekness says you are one who submits your _____ to those in

  authority over you. By keeping your temper and emotions under _____, and not

  _____ yourself in heated confrontations, you allow others to _____

  this fruit they see in you.

- **Temperance (Self-control)**

  The Greek means having the personality of restraint and control over your _____,

  _____, and _____. Think about how your control over yourself stands.

  How's your _____, your _____, your

  _____ and _____? With this Fruit of the Spirit as a

  character in your life, you can be pleased with your _____ of life and know you can be

  a good _____ to others.

Now That This is All Said

We know we cannot do anything without God and the help of the Holy Spirit. You have to ask the Holy Spirit to

_____ you grow good fruit, _____, _____, and

_____. Growing any fruit in the natural needs the basic elements of

_____, _____, and _____. It is the same in the spiritual.

These are provided in your Bible. Take advantage of all the free gifts provided therein. You will become a

_____ Christian who can lead others into _____ and

_____.

SO JUST DO IT!